A Gal's Guide To Finessing Life

Mayalyn Hardee

Dedicated to all the girls and women. Let my mistakes,
triumphs, and transparency be a lamp for your feet.

Contents

Introduction

 Have you ever wanted to 'fix' your life and even taken some initial steps but kept finding yourself in the same spot? Some people are lucky enough to have mentors or coaches lecturing them on the difference between goals and dreams. Dreams can't be measured in actions, but a goal has quantifiable steps that inch you closer and closer to the finish line. Let's pretend for a moment that you already knew this concept and have witnessed yourself inching towards and even crossing the finish line for several goals! Then why didn't that solve your feeling of inadequate fulfillment? Because you still needed to learn *the truth*!

Your life is like a bento box. Have you ever seen one of those?

Illustration by Joan Fodor

The different compartments of this Japanese lunchbox make up the whole, but the contents are separated into their own quadrants. *Spirituality; Hygiene, Beauty and Wellness; Relationships with Others;* and *Coinz* are foundational categories of your being that must be poured into from moment to moment.

Once you optimize how to manage yourself, you'll achieve a soft life of fulfillment and operate like a boss chick. Some bento boxes have equally sized sections, but that's like a slow and steady wins the race kind of thing; for a fast life of explosive results occurring all the time, your bento box should dedicate one section to be much bigger than the others.

"You remind me of Rihanna. I know you favor her looks, but your aura. I met Rihanna once, and she is a deeply spiritual woman. So powerful."

- Dr. Kimberley

This book will identify the four quadrants, how they lead to a life of fulfillment, and will require you to imagine what you want your life to look like.

You'll be called to examine where your expectations are even coming from. Are you gleaming with desire for images you see in media? Perhaps some things you've read or the descriptions of romance and monetary successes you've heard in songs or movies.

Your five senses: taste, touch, sight, smell, and hearing are responsible for most of your input. You're constantly being programmed by your external environment. Unless you expressly declare a hierarchal order of which influence has authority to dictate, you and whoever's attached to you will be tossed to and fro.

Burning embers of thoughts fall, hoping to land somewhere to combust into a flame and set materials on fire. This can work in your favor if you are conscious and understand the benefits of a controlled fire. (Firefighters identify things that would typically go up in flames in a wildfire and burn them ahead of time as a preventative measure against disaster).

What people have named "feelings" and "emotions" always follow thoughts.

Beware of your thoughts, for they become words.

Beware of your words, for they become actions.

Beware of your actions, for they become habits.

Beware of your habits, for they become character.

Beware of your character, for it becomes your destiny.

"My feelings ain't as strong as my mind *NEVER."

-Moneybagg Yo

Train your mind to gate-keep what enters into it. All you are exposed to contributes to one or many sections of your bento box, and you are the executive chef. Which of the areas should be the largest? If you want your life to catapult, place your bets on *Spirituality*.

When your spiritual routine is regularly followed, it's like having a cheat code. Everything else in your other categories flows potently like mini fireworks, splashes of extra sauce, and quicker results than ever!

Whichever section you invest in most doesn't change the fact that all those quadrants are essential!

Hygiene, Beauty and Wellness influence self-esteem and how others perceive you. *Relationships with Others* and your navigations therein identify you in society. *Coinz* is the self-help, educational, and financial part of yourself that opens doors for opportunities to build prosperity. Can you see any of those spearheading your existence?

If dressing well with soft skin and angel baby breath is the lead, is that enough of a driving force to assist the other 3 categories toward your self-actualization? Well, they work in tandem with each other, but truthfully, no category except *Spirituality* runs anything.

Now, walk through that hypothetical:

Lead with *Hygiene, Beauty and Wellness* to decide in *Coinz* which captivating domain name to create for your new business idea. You're a hottie, so you use your sex appeal and bomb looks to get advice from your CEO boyfriend. WINNING! You get a rush from the experience and feel powerful, limitless even! He also agreed to partner with you and invest.

Seems like this should be the most significant section in the bento! Okay, so keep going:

You've invested significant efforts into your *Hygiene, Beauty and Wellness*; thus, your aesthetics allow you to be kind and empathetic towards others since you are so fortunate, and accustomed to gaining favor. People cater to you, you have no hesitation in catering to them; thus, your *Relationships with Others* thrive. But will this help you in scenarios like setting boundaries with family members?

Fear usually characterizes an inability to advocate for oneself, and if you've struggled with this your whole life, looking cute may not be the solution. Although a lot can be said about a person who keeps up with their looks, like discipline and consistency, does that translate into you saying no when your aunt asks to borrow money for the millionth time without repayment? Being beautiful is not an all-encompassing solution to life.

The question becomes, is life all about balancing everything, or can one area receive the majority investment and predicate the successes of the rest of you?

Throughout this text, you'll get advice tailored to the four quadrants. By exploring what each quadrant comprises and the benefits therein, you will come to the knowledge of two principles:

1. *To achieve fullness of self, you must develop a lifestyle of consistent maintenance of your four cubicles. Lacking in one will reveal deleterious effects.*

2. *You can have it all, but without conscious pursuit and awareness of your Spirituality, your fulfillment cannot be sustained.*

If number two is intimidating, don't let that seed of thought develop into anxiety or fear. Creating a spiritual awareness is easier than you think, and you will get to that part of the book much later. Keep your hands inside (or out!) the ride at all times, and please enjoy your journey.

How To Read This Book

~

Interpret this text as if someone in your best interest is giving you their advice from personal experiences, but understand they are human and don't have all the answers. Some things may come across as preachy, while others are suggestive. Still, you are entering an experience with great learning potential.

Some things will resonate now, but others will only be applicable once you're in another season of your life. At the same time, even some concepts may turn you off altogether. Push through. If a section seems overwhelming, skip it and go to another page. You don't have to read it from front to back; instead, pick out random pages with optimism that something will speak to your soul and inspire the changes you want to see!

The perspective you're reading is from an attractive 35-year-old woman who grew up in a Christian family with traditions and values. While identifying as a Christian from an early age, the conduct you'll read about has not always followed that, and in fact, will show a breaking away from those values, particularly in the discussion about sexuality and relationships.

Attractive, well-paid and generous older gentlemen tended to gravitate; many situations that should've been departed from resulted in abuse from clouded judgment, a lack of common sense, and rebelling against good counsel. Ultimately, a return to biblical principles and a renewed intimate relationship with Christ emerged and made all the difference. The goal is not to be indoctrinated but rather to learn and interpret lessons so you can make even better decisions.

Personal development is a rollercoaster lifestyle change that can make you feel like you're all over the place. Understand, your progress in one quadrant may not mirror that of another.

The mess that you are is absolutely epic and unique. You are 1 of 1 on this planet, so enjoy the ride and congratulate yourself for even caring to become a better version of yourself. As you grow and recognize your trends and habits, lead with love and gentleness in your self-talk.

You may sometimes feel uncomfortable, but if you follow through with this program, all your dreams will eventually come true. More importantly, what you dream about will evolve to higher levels, and you will become equipped to take action for others, all while living a saucy, fly life of lacking nothing. One of the best feelings in the world is to have what you love and then learn that it's eternally yours! Get into it...

QUADRANT 1

Relationships with Others

≈

This quadrant is all about interacting with other humans. To succeed in life, you must figure out various types of verbal and nonverbal communication, physical interactions, and being the director of your mind.

1. Alignment

The rules of engagement for relationships have evolved, particularly with the emergence of texting and social media. In youth, you're taught to be courteous in speech with thank you's and please's and asking permission before eating the last piece of cake. You achieve a particular response by using those pleasantries, but there's also something to be desired by being edgy and mysterious. You'll learn that being a teacher's pet may get you better grades, but will you be invited to the sleepover?

What do you want, and where are the people who also like those things? When you align with like-minded individuals, you waste less time explaining yourself and more time living. There's no right way to navigate relationships; it depends on the outcome you desire. How has technology changed things? If you open someone's message and leave them on 'read,' that's considered 'shots fired.' If you're going to not reply to someone, they may slowly stop reaching out to you. So don't be a dinosaur; learn some phone hacks to help you carefully navigate those relationships and generally stick with people who approach technology like you. If you don't massage your friendships, their nature will change, and you may lose access to the benefits of the original dynamic; you have to deposit to withdraw from the relationship. If everyone is talking about the TikTok trend, and you're annoyed because 'social media brainwashes,' know that *you're* actually being the oddball, not them.

Each relationship requires its own objective. You may want to be promoted or treated with respect by your employer. There is a particular set of behaviors for you to adhere to. With your parents, perhaps you want them to see you as exceptional and reliable. This will dictate your tone of voice, the actions you avoid and engage in, and your methods of communication. No relationship is exempt from the required attention that's called for, even with your pet. If you want your puppy to sit when your voice produces the command, it will take consistent facial expressions, gestures, and other such efforts. This also applies to your relationship with yourself, but more of that will come in the *Spirituality* chapter.

It must be restated: Your conduct in varying types of relationships may differ, but the required attention that's called for is never exempt. If you look at a cross-section of your romantic, familial, and professional relationships, you'll notice a current that interconnects them all. That current is you. Your thoughts, actions, habits, and character shine through consistently.

"More Than a One-Night Stand

His name was Yelleh (pronounced Yell-aye!), and he was everything. Thick, dangerously dark eyebrows, a dominant and Israeli-accented voice, and his beard was the age I loved, the early forties. The club had been bangin'! Jak was my newest right hand, and she shared my sentiments then. At 3:18 a.m., we were seated. It was grub time at Berri's, Beverly Hills' hottest pizza spot.

During the week, Berri's was easily approachable, but on the weekend late at night, its dance music blared, and the line wrapped down the block. The valet was full of luxury whips, and being two hot girls was the persuasive element that got you seated right away. I ordered soup.

Jak and I had been introduced by a progressive thinker, and our connection was made instantly. Two kind hearts were practicing lessons of being direct.

'Soup? I've yet to meet a girl drinking soup here. My name is Daniel, if there's anything you need, it's yours. I own the place, so you just let me know.'

I smiled softly, then smoothly broke away from the hypnotizing stare to turn back towards Jak. She looked graceful and poised. The perfect wing-woman.

After she affirmed that he was gone, I smiled hard, and she eagerly returned it. Ten minutes later, the server returned *to tell us our bill had been taken care of as Dan-yelleh reappeared and asked me to go away with him for the night. 'Tell me the address of your friend. I will have a driver safely take her home.' 'If you come with me you will be paid $4,000 cash. You and I will party.'*

True to who I was in that instance, I excitedly asked my friend if she was cool with it and went away with him that night.

It was a whirlwind romance, which, in hindsight, was not the best idea. Dan-yelleh was my passionate love interest who exposed me to influence and agonizing heartache that I had to unpack for many years after that. I loved him. But that's beside the point.

Jak's willingness to adjust her night's itinerary indebted me to my relationship with her in the best way. It made me aspire to be a supportive, flexible friend like her. Henceforth, I always sought friendships that mirrored that scene. The following day, she called to check on me, passed no judgment, and looked forward to going out together again.

The takeaway is the importance of a) knowing the fabric of who you are and b) being in the company of people aligned with that so fluidity, cherishing, and respect can be experienced by all involved parties from moment to moment. Then everybody's happy!"

— *Journal Entry, 2000s*

Who you are accompanies you everywhere. If you know that specific scenarios will compel you to behave a particular way, you'll learn to go out with girls who are okay with catching a ride home. The type of friends who will be poised and elegant when you need them as a marketing approach. Friends who won't be envious or resentful and sensitive to abandonment. When you know who you are, you can communicate confidently with people to learn who they are.

Find your tribe, and you'll spend much less time explaining yourself. They'll get it, and that synergy will allow you all to experience the fullness of life in safe spaces. You'll have people to talk to when things go awry because fear of judgment won't be a thing. Vulnerability increases intimacy, but it's also true that you must guard your heart "....for everything you do flows from it" (Proverbs 4:23 NIV). By the way, anytime a word with numbers and abbreviations follow, this is a scripture reference to the Holy Bible.

What if you discover that the person you're with is not aligned with your behavioral tendencies? Determine if a value exchange can be exercised between you two, and curate your hangouts. Avoid settings that detract from the relationship characteristics you deem worthwhile. If you're in a scenario where you find yourself choosing between what you want and what they want, some advice may be to put on your own oxygen mask before placing on theirs.

What matters is how you will feel about yourself later if you're willing to disappoint your friends and are comfortable being at risk of losing that friendship altogether. These decisions are often made in microseconds or may be made over several hours of deliberation. Consider the ramifications of you possibly hurting this person's feelings and/or triggering their sensitivities. Also, weigh if the opportunity you are oscillating between is worth the gamble! Maybe you sacrifice one decision, and from that experience, you learn and declare to yourself, the next time to choose better!

Your intuition will do the brunt of the work for you in all situations, which is why your bento box should have an extra large spot for *Spirituality*. Logic and analysis go a long way, but wisdom eliminates inner conflict. The best way to ensure the highest vibrational outcome for any situation within all relationships is not to solely apply rules of engagement. Rather instill trust in the Holy Spirit to lead its sheep to safety.

In relationships, you should do what suits the other person *and* yourself. When all parties hold that duty, relationships flourish. How will you know there's an imbalance?

Observing the other person choose themself over you all the time can be hurtful unless they choose themselves as much as you choose yourself. You may desire entirely *giving* relationships, and your cousin may only give so much before exhibiting selfishness. Do you cut that relationship off? Cutting someone's access to you is not a bad idea in many cases. Some people have friendships dating back to the 2nd grade, which is beautiful. Forming new bonds isn't always easy and requires much work and patience. Consider that when you desire to sever a relationship and determine if you can instead re-categorize it. If this person gossips often, consider sharing your secrets with someone else yet still enjoy trips to the mall and the other beautiful intersecting interests.

It takes a lot of concentrated energy and sacrifice to achieve sustainable change. Do you know what repentance means? It's to change. Not to apologize but to be different. Many people are not going to. When they tell you who they are, believe them. Let that sink in.

As you continue to be who you are, understand which battles you are willing to fight and which things you can let go of. What is your purpose? To convince the other person to yield to your will? To help them achieve a better understanding of you? To learn more about them? Sometimes, being your entire self is too much for the other person to accept in relationships. What do you do? Never shrink. You can strategize, though. You don't always have to voice your opinion on a topic. Save that opinion and bless someone else with it, someone who will house and appreciate the expressions of your mind.

2. Boundaries

In the context of romantic relationships, how do boundaries apply? Knowing oneself is the key to all relationship types. An awareness of your triggers, biases, and desires contributes to the necessary formation of your boundaries. Even the tremendous force of the ocean operates within limits.

> *"...He gave the sea its boundary so the waters would not overstep his command..."*
>
> **— Proverbs 8:29 NIV**

Devastation is evident in catastrophic occurrences wherein oceans wash upon shores to flood villages and swallow livelihoods. In that same regard, consider that the force inside people is comparable to planets in orbit; would you want a world without bounds to collide with you? Surely not if damage ensues, but what about that planet nestling up close to you, penetrating your layers a little bit at a time? This is the type of interaction that can cause detriment. It seems unassuming and casual; however, worlds are merging without boundaries. Mr. Hardee explained this concept to his daughter and it changed her approach to relationships.

You associate tsunamis with violent force and collision, but in the case of energetic exchange, imagine the occurrence of a slow-motion version. When you speak your truth to someone who does not celebrate your contributions, you are violently assaulted each time they diminish you with their self-proclaimed "real-ism." By projecting their own visions of you onto you, they limit the universe that you are! It would be best if you taught people how to treat you and for you to know your hard lines.

A hard line is where you have zero tolerance for behavior at its first sighting and afford no additional opportunities for the other party to exhibit change. Your hard line is often developed from experiences of pain, which encourage your autonomous nervous system to flee at the hint of any subsequent occurrences, and sometimes they are taught to you by either a mentor, coach or parental figure. Otherwise, people deduce that they should prevent certain things from happening by learning horror stories from others or a moral code known through philosophy or religion. There are many ways to learn how to develop boundaries and expectations for behavior, and you are encouraged to know them because boundaries predicate survival.

"Hey, Niah, do you agree communication is responsible for 80% of the success you will have in life?"

"I say comprehension! You can communicate all day, but if the person can't comprehend, then…"

—a discussion with Niah

Creating the boundary is one thing: DO not speak to me this way.

But how do you enforce it? Many people know what triggers them and have declared that they don't like it and won't put up with it. Yet they'll complain and feel perplexed about it, with no foreseeable solution. The key is knowing thyself. You are valuable. You deserve to be cherished or respected by everyone, measured by honoring your boundaries. When you know this about you, you will be willing to walk boldly away from whomever is not complicit. If you aren't sure and decide to remain, remember the visual of a slow-motion Tsunami and know that's what is occurring.

Be BOLD and unapologetic when you are both establishing your limitations and expressing them. "I think you shouldn't come over unannounced anymore" differs significantly from "I do not accept unannounced visitors; please respect my boundary and do not do it again." When that person does it again, because sometimes they do, let there be consequences. Don't answer the door, block their call, or call a voice of authority, even if that voice is a police officer! What you want matters. In that same way, you should respect the boundaries of others.

It would help to find out what makes people tick and identify what stops that clock. Individuals operate from varying life experiences, standards of conduct, and mindsets. You'll pick up on a lot when you pay attention to the details of their relationships with others, speech, and body language. Most communication is non-verbal, so as much as you should observe *others*, remember they are watching *you*. For example, if you constantly share others' secrets, they will consider that you will share theirs. Relationships are constant interviews, and all parties have the authority to remove themselves at any given time. So, enjoy each moment with others as if it's your last because tomorrow is not promised!

Now that it's established that all relationship types rely on communicated boundaries, what is the difference between romantic, platonic, familial, and professional relationships? There are rules of engagement for each one, but also tailored to the people involved. If your boo always pays for all the dates in a romantic relationship, that may be fine. But imagine always offering to pay for the bill when out with your friend, and them always letting you. Oh, burn! Or, you go on a date, and your boo asks to split the bill! Do you automatically friend-zone them? There is no golden rule that goes across all relationships in that regard. Still, it's essential to learn your preferences so when the moments present, you'll be ready and willing to speak up or act accordingly. You're trying to avoid consistently experiencing uncomfortableness or being poorly diminished in the long run. Remember, each interaction with anyone either adds to or detracts from you in the spiritual exchange. You are not your body; you are in your body having an experience.

Most of your education about relationship conduct will be through observation and trial and error, although some people hire situational coaches! To be a good person, you should always do what's suitable for yourself and consider what's right for the other person. When there are multiple persons involved, a clear prioritization comes in handy.

3. Relationship Hierarchy

〜

Relationship Hierarchy involves honesty about which relationships are most important to you in case you approach a crossroads. You may have to choose between loyalties, and it would be great to know where you stand in advance. Your sister may be at war with your boyfriend, or you may have become great friends with your employer or boss, who just indicated she would fire your co-worker. Do you tell the colleague secretly and betray your boss, or simply mind your business? Whose friendship do you value the most? A Likert Scale is handy in this case.

"Honey, you oscillate between choices a lot. You're my best friend, so there's obviously no judgment, and I also acknowledge that these epiphanies you reach about your relationship with him are cyclical. Would you consider making a Likert Scale to determine your feelings about your situation?"

-Ashley

This type of measurement assigns a number value to a trait, and once you sum up the numbers, it is an excellent indicator of worth. It's a better alternative to a comparative scale wherein you assign just one value; all items are not created equally, and that should be accounted for. If that sounds confusing, check out this example:

The first scale lists how satisfied you are with the contributions of both your boss and coworker. It asks for a satisfaction value on a scale from 1-5, with 5 being the greatest:

Person of Interest	Their Contribution	Satisfaction Value 1-5
Boss	Pays Me	5
	Gave Me A Raise	5
	Will Write A Referral	5
		Total: 15
Co-worker	Gives Beauty Tips	5
	Has Lunch With Me	5
	Sound Board For Advice	5
		Total: 15

Contrastingly, the Likert Scale assigns a varying and appropriate value of worth to the item and how satisfied you are with it:

Person of Interest	Their Contribution	Satisfaction Value 1-5
Boss	Pays Me	10/10
	Gave Me A Raise	3/3
	Will Write A Referral	7/7
		Total: 20
Co-worker	Gives Beauty Tips	5/5
	Has Lunch With Me	2/2
	Sound Board For Advice	10/10
		Total: 17

In the first chart all things are measured equally, and both parties score 15 points respectively. Contrastingly, in the second chart, notice the value assigned is a more accurate depiction of how much something is worth.

Hypothetically, you assign payment as 10 points because that's very valuable. A raise is only 3 points because it's nice but isn't crucial to your current lifestyle. Finally, 7 points go to a referral.

For your Co-worker, beauty tips are great but only worth 5 pts. Lunch companionship is fantastic, but other co-workers offer this, so 2 points. Contrastingly, her advice helps you tremendously, so you give it a high 10 points.

Based on this scale, the boss totals a value of 20 points, while Co-worker only scored 17. Cut and dry, emotions to the side, seems like you should find a way to mind your business!

The reality is you'll want to be successful in all of the relationships that affect your daily life and your world. You may seek a compromise, which, in this example, could look like you giving your co-worker lots of positive affirmations about how capable and brilliant she is and can work any occupation in her field. Things that give her a confidence boost, which will come in handy when she is terminated. There are many ways to work the system, but ultimately, your priorities will keep you organized and dictate how to manage various dynamics. You can protect yourself from emotional heartache if you are clear on your motivations and willing to stand tall in the outcomes, consequences, and blessings.

4. Expectations

～

The key to successful relationships with others is being transparent about the values all parties bring to the table. The assessment is a two-way street; while you note what they have, please believe your contribution is just as evaluated. Determine which qualities are imperative in your relationships and evaluate potential new associates through those lenses. Perhaps they bring a contribution you never knew you needed! How stunningly amazing that is! Like life, relationships are breathing and alive, not rigid and inflexible. Discern which qualities are the foundation of your relationships, those non-negotiable must-haves, and allow the other qualities to be additions.

The difference between an addition and a foundational attribute is that you hold the latter in the highest regard, and while other qualities may be necessary, their coming and going may not be deal breakers for you. If someone approaches you with addition qualities, you'll allow yourself to be excited, but you will remain observant. Don't automatically render your qualification stamp before those foundational qualities are confirmed. Allowing someone into your social network without granting access to your inner circle is okay.

As relationships evolve, expectations may as well. Loyalty could be expected at the beginning of a 4-year relationship, but by year 4, disloyalty may be a deal breaker. Ideally, dialogues would ensue throughout the connection to check in about what has changed and what remains. If someone starts off always giving well-received advice, and now the receiver has graduated to a point where they no longer welcome unsolicited opinions, that could leave the giver feeling displaced. What do you do with that displacement? Talk about it.

"I noticed that you love to give advice, and lately, I haven't needed any and have asked you to stop offering it. Is there another way we can think of for you to express your helpful and assistive energy in my direction? How about you help me pick out the linen for my new house? I really do value your advice!"

Having two 'woke' people in a relationship is great, but sometimes even one has the skills to elevate both. The less woke individual has a choice: either rise to the occasion and evolve or diminish you in their minds. By minimizing you, they won't have to deal with the growing pains associated with the prospect of leveling up. This is an unfortunate action some people take, but lots of people actually elevate instead!

What was once an addition expectation can migrate to being a foundational one, and vice versa. You may have required impeccable oral hygiene as a foundational aspect, then learned through experience that severely lacking emotional intelligence (EQ) would change your perspective. Having your feelings crushed by the one who smiled and breathed their deliciously minty breath on you, and you learned that although you value both, EQ was foundational and mandatory. You needed more of it than the other qualities.

Everyone functions differently and has varying things that keep them going. Your contributions are being evaluated, and you may think you are irreplaceable by offering a foundational trait. Still, you never know which ratio a person desires at any given moment. As previously stated, dialogue goes a long way in figuring that out. Ultimately, by being self-aware, consistent, and ever-evolving, you will bring your highest version of self, and what more could be asked of you than that?

5. Controlling Tendencies

"Expecting people to do what you would do in a situation only leads to your disappointment, not theirs. They go on living their lives. So let people be who they are; you accept or reject it."

—Adrienne Doan

Many people will not change; here's a tip on how to change or control them: You can't.

Your desire likely stems from your dislike of their behavior because it violates your personal boundaries. Perhaps you are emotionally triggered by some of their actions and comprehend that 'If they would just stop doing XYZ, everything would be great.' Being aware of your own HALT will assist you with your triggers and bring the authority over your emotions back into your hands.

HALT is an acronym coined by Dr. Charles Stanley, which stands for Hungry, Angry or Annoyed, Lonely, and Tired. He recommends to never react or analyze situations while in one of those non-regulated states because you will not be in control of yourself. Half your battles are due to inadequate states of mind, body, and soul. If you are satiated, in a positive mood, have your love tank filled, and are well rested, you'll view things differently and have a higher threshold for irritation. If you nurture your fundamental equilibrium, the triggering will drastically decrease.

Go back to trying to control your relationships with others and why this doesn't work: Think of a young toddler throwing a tantrum and flinging themself to the floor in disarray. From the outside looking in, you may think 'that kid needs to get ahold of themself and behave!' But neuroscience points to another view.

The prefrontal cortex is the brain's front part that is responsible for emotional regulation. This is not fully developed in an adult person until the age of 25, so imagine what it's like for a two-year-old. The limbic system is where your primitive emotions reside. Messages of anger, sadness, annoyance, etc., are born there and even reptiles have such a basic system.

The limbic system does not care about your long-term goals or relationships with others, only how you feel in the moment. Self-awareness means observing yourself when triggered and acknowledging your feelings. This produces activity in the prefrontal cortex, which determines if something is worth reacting to or not, thus growing self-control and mindfulness.

The simple act of being self-aware when in a heightened emotional state reduces its negative impact! Be observant and responsible about your HALT. How does this connect to controlling your partner? Well, discussing a little more about the brain answers this question.

The brain processes information by forming a network of specialized nerve cells called neurons. For these many neurons to communicate with each other, messages are passed through connections in the brain called synapses.

If you look at the image of a human brain from birth to adulthood, you'll see that at 2 years old, the baby's brain has twice as many synapses as the adult's. Depending on a child's experiences, some synapses are strengthened through repeated use, while others rarely used are eliminated through pruning. By the time you become an adult, you have reinforced synapses that encourage you to behave and respond in specific ways. This is all determined by your childhood and adolescent experiences. Learning, memory, and other cognitive abilities are all predicated by the input our brain receives from the environment.

You are wired one way, and your partner is wired another way. Something that may seem basic and easily adaptable to you may be the exact opposite for them. The more you learn about your friend's childhood and adolescence, the more insight you'll gain into their actions and inactions.

Threatening, manipulating, and pleading are sometimes futile if your partner's brain is hardwired against what you want them to do; things may or may not ever change. You can't force things; you can only be clear about *your* boundaries, tolerances, and communication. Being accountable for your triggers and responses and ensuring you are self-aware of your HALT will provide you a much better life experience than plotting how to change an entirely different human being.

Maximum excellence in *Relationships with Others* gives you a reliable network you can lean on for support. There are many benefits to knowing how to navigate communication, including not ending a relationship that helps to balance you simply because the other party does something that happens to be your pet peeve.

Some people ignite the fire in your soul, giving you just the pep talk you need to power through your day or that bear hug that renders you loving support instantaneously. The cousin who can seemingly read your mind when you two burst into laughter upon locking eyes contributes to your homeostasis and should be treated preciously. You are responsible for doing what's suitable for the other person and not abusing or betraying them. If you all care for each other that way, you'll encounter agape love, a wonderful transcendent experience.

Don't commit to the person who is imperfect and ever-evolving; instead, commit to the relationships you forge with boundaries, honest and prompt communication, and vulnerability.

6. Yin and Yang

Dr. Scott Hays is a valuable mentor who explained the following concept: Each person in a relationship harbors two selves: the masculine yin and feminine yang. For energetic alignments, a Waltz dance must occur; one person steps forward while the other steps backward, and then vice versa. If you find yourself constantly taking steps forward, that's not right. If you're always taking steps backward, it's also not okay. Dance the vibe of energetic exchanges.

Everything is energy-based, even conversation. You may think of an interaction with someone and not recall what they said, but how they made you feel. Before speaking, get your consciousness right, prepare to meet someone, and don't be an empty performer. Expand around that person, set the stage for the interaction, and be intentional about what sentiment you want that person to walk away with.

Also, know that the other party is doing the same with you consciously or unconsciously. Guard yourself from energy vampires and pessimistic vibes, but remain open to enjoying invigorating exchanges!

The other categories of life balance can sometimes become neglected once you are enthralled with one particular relationship or even all of them. Social obligations can usurp your time, and a few days off from fitness, skincare, or meditation can quickly snowball into an altered routine. Beware of significant changes in your routine, mainly if those changes leave you experiencing H.A.L.T or any other detrimental effects.

Mutual obsession is often sought because it feels the safest for our emotions and vulnerabilities, but sometimes, it can swallow and spit you out. Co-dependence is unhealthy because it means independently you're not okay with yourself, and you need an outside source for joy. You had your routine for a reason. Throwing it all away for that person is fun and lovely, and seemingly romantic. This will likely lead to resentment of them in the future if you are unhappy with who you have become.

Some relationships are perfect; you'll feel like your heart finally has a home. The person will mirror your qualities while introducing you to their other lovely ones. If you feel like you need to change parts of yourself in order to be accepted and kept by them, then this is an indication of co-dependence. In a healthy dynamic, you will be able to be yourself fully and not fear abandonment by the other person.

"You've literally seen every side of me and every mood I could possibly have…you should be offended you even know me, haha, yet we're best friends."

—Niah

If you meet someone like that, find a way to hold on to them, it's just priceless. You will experience significant regret if you mishandle or abandon those sweet individuals.

7. Stages of Relationship

〰️

There are 4 stages of a relationship, each calling for your attention. *Meeting, Honeymoon, Enlightenment, and Commitment. Meeting* is just as the name suggests. *Honeymoon* is when things are sugar, spice, and everything nice. Later, usually after 1 to 2 quarters (or 3-6 months), is *Enlightenment,* where the ugly traits everyone's been hiding start to surface and perhaps cause conflicts. That stage usually breaks or makes the relationship.

Next, both parties enter the *Commitment* stage when it's decided that things can still work or even thrive between them. What a series of processes! All stages are demanding, but particularly *Enlightenment.* You attract what you are, and whoever that is will mirror both your darkness and your light. When push comes to shove during the *Enlightenment* stage, you may notice yourself becoming judgmental or particularly perturbed with traits in your best friend. Sometimes, they are not the problem!

Before you throw the entire relationship away, identify if the things you see in them are merely things you dislike about yourself. What if you create space with grace and understanding towards that person, a grace you would appreciate being given to you when you're being an idiot? As an alternative, push the person away and cut off contact.

The problem is that you can run but can't hide from yourself. You will continue to meet the same people until you heal your heart, so are they the problem, or are you? What can be learned in self-discovery from your observations and interactions with them? If you become a runner, you're delaying your own growth. This doesn't mean staying in an unhealthy dynamic, but first try boundary setting before trashing the whole thing; In some cases it's better to cut off complete contact and do it quickly. That's where ghosting happens. Ghosting is when someone severs communication, often without warning, and makes it difficult for you to ever find them again. It hurts to be the one who gets ghosted, but never take it personally. If you must get away from someone quickly, that's a reflection of you and your needs, and you should act on that confidently. Lingering past your due date is a betrayal of self, and it will eventually end in a heartache that you're delaying.

"We all know how relationships are. Not one person can be everything to another person. It doesn't mean you need someone on the side, but you have to have your own activities. It can't always be "I love you, I love you" and fairytales. There are real-world things to be dealt with."

—RE

There are achievable fairytales with beautiful endings. When it works out, great!; but when it doesn't, it's essential to navigate recovery from disappointments healthily. Proper healing allows you to get back out there and attract exactly what you want for next time.

8. The Four Rules of BREAKUPS

i. [Assess]ing Fulfillment of needs
ii. [Be]ing Around Loved Ones
iii. [Becom]ing Poppin'
iv. [Bounc]ing back

Breakups are like deaths; some connection to another person is severed, affecting the psyche, emotions, and behaviors. Society downplays these significant events, and even when depicted in movies, the devastation that can occur only lasts a few scenes, followed by some happy ending. If a breakup is not approached correctly, the long-term damage can kill a person's ability to perceive love (plus, they'll waste a lot of time dwelling). Sticking to the four rules cuts all the crap and gives you the roadmap to get through the breakup beating with reduced injuries; You'll achieve a clear idea of how to move forward and an expedited route to self-fulfillment. You've cried long enough.

i. Assess[ing] the Fulfillment of Your Needs

A proper assessment of your needs is crucial since it gives you a realistic perspective of what's going on. You may think you have a clear vision, but emotions can't be trusted during breakups.

Your job is to jot down everything you want. Examples include an allowance, someone to cuddle with, a new hairstyle, exercise, learning about the stock market. You want to make sure you're not limiting yourself here. This list, once completed, should draw your attention to the big picture. Often, breakups make you feel worthless and drained. You've convinced yourself that you lost the most important thing in your life and nothing else matters. That's simply an illusion and you will overcome!

Now that you have a list, write down your ex friend or ex romantic partner's name next to the items they contributed to. If they didn't do much for you, keep that in mind when assessing your loss. Are you romanticizing and exaggerating their impact in your life? In some cases, that ex did a lot for you, so now it's time to make a new list of everyone else in your life, and what they contribute to your well-being.

Sara: Flowers, workout buddy, jokes.

Brandon: Pays the mortgage, has good companionship.

Oliver: Sends daily bible verses.

If you aren't very social and only have yourself to list, that's okay, too. Write down everything you contribute to yourself.

Me: I give positive reinforcement, attend yoga, clean up, and watch movies.

By now, hopefully you're noticing that you bring a lot to the table for your own self just by being alive and conscious each day. You have an awareness that a network plays just as important a role to bring you joyous moments. If not, then that's an area for you to work on in building connections. The main point, is to not be completely dependent an another person emotionally.

If it turns out that your ex was excellent in fulfilling all or the majority of your needs, this reveals which mindset you should have during the breakup:

- A plan for reconciliation.
- A plan for achieving closure.

There's nothing wrong with wanting to repair the relationship, but you must realize that sometimes the other person needs time. Other times, the other person just isn't interested. That's hard to swallow because it puts the ball in their court and leaves you feeling helpless. Hoping for reconciliation means you should refrain from saying the wrong thing in the aftermath of the breakup. When you're sad or angry, the impulse is to shut the person out entirely or threaten that they should hurry up and come back. Both incite rage in the other person and lead to more sadness for you. Instead of emailing, texting, or calling, record what you want to say for yourself. This gets it off your chest without affecting the other person. Also, a recording shows you what your emotion looks like so you can adjust it as necessary.

You can't force the other person whether you want to reconcile or not. Even if you want nothing to do with your ex, you can't erase the past or force an apology from them. Instead, it would be best if you always aimed for healthy closure. In the meantime, write a letter to your ex that you will never send. Start with the highlights of the relationship, then talk about what sucked, and conclude with a heartfelt goodbye.

DO NOT SEND THE LETTER. It's essential to get all of your feelings on paper. This exercise does wonders in providing closure; it doesn't mean there's no hope of getting back together; it psychologically relieves you.

Any friendship or relationship's ultimate outcome is learning more about oneself. Write down or record what you learned about your strengths, weaknesses, and habits from your experience. The sooner you realize and accept that every instance is a part of your destiny to prepare you for the next thing, the less pain you will feel.

What you are feeling is real! No one can tell you to get over it. It's your process. Each tear, ache, and sleepless night is another reminder that you are human. You will be surprised at how many people on the planet are experiencing the exact same feelings at the same time as you. Be realistic about what fulfills you, and know you will be fulfilled again! Go easy on yourself, and follow each step in your process.

ii. [Be]ing Around Loved Ones

Isolation feels like a great idea, but the second rule is that you must be around people to absorb new energy. What if you only have access to mutual friends or people who give terrible advice? In this case, you're still not off the hook. Go to the mall, online chat room, or hotel lobby and start mingling! Rule #2 is super important, so if you don't have anyone, go online and look up positive affirmations related to your needs. Turn up the volume and allow that author to fill your ears because there's no excuse for carelessly not following this step.

Being around people may seem intolerable, especially if you are constantly on the verge of tears. However, human interaction normalizes your existence. You can talk about the relationship if it makes you feel better, but hearing about someone else's life may provide a break from obsessing over your situation. If you're lucky and have a girlfriend who will gas you up and tell you how wonderful you are and that you deserve the best, then you are truly blessed. These girls will infuse your self-esteem by reminding you of what they love about you. Just because one relationship failed doesn't mean you'll feel bad forever.

"My friend, I call the Oldengay Erbvay (That's Pig Latin, by the way) instinctively would call me when I was at my absolute lowest. She has this internal compass that points to me whenever I feel pathetic. After about 4 minutes on the

phone with her, I feel like a bunch of layers get shed off of me, and I am lighter, more confident, and bouncier. She'd say, 'If you saw you the way I see you, you'd be cat-walking through your living room. Is that the girl with the green eyes who has her own business? Am I talking to the top model who never drops her chin, bosses up in every category, and attracts everything she wants from life? Is that you? Because that's the queen I called, the one whose prayer changes lives for her people and can't be stopped! That's you, right? Okay, yass queen!' How can you not be lifted from despair when you get a phone call like that?!"

— Journal Entry, 2020

Family can be helpful, too, since they will have known you way longer than your ex and can take you down memory lane, making you laugh or transporting you mentally to a different place. Volunteering to help someone helps you stay active and gives you endorphins from feeling useful. Take a walk downtown. Be around people you don't know. Observe and feel alive. If you can help it, surround yourself with people who are enthusiastic about life. Individuals who have good fortune and optimism. They'll tell you there are plenty of opportunities to meet new fish in the sea, and you'll roll your eyes. Of course, you've heard this before and are not impressed, but that's fine! What matters is that you are hearing it!

"I knew you wouldn't be up until about 12 noon, but I figured you'd be hungry when you came downstairs. There's some breakfast on the stove for you. You'll be alright."

-Papa Carl Standley

It's great to watch a comedy, but even a romance film will help you to heal. You'll find similarities between your relationship and those in the script. This will get your tears flowing, which is a healthy mechanism. Imploding and suppressing have long-term adverse effects; let it out! There is an alternative if you don't have the liberty or desire to be around loved ones. Begin a new activity or project. Endorphins are released when you immerse yourself in developing a new skill, giving you pleasure. Even if it is something you haven't done in a while, it's still somewhat new to you. This can be solo or with friends. Music can be like a loved one since it talks to you and hears your emotions. Take yourself to another reality by playing music you used to jam out to when you were happy, and things were going your way. Too many love songs could lead you down the wrong path; play some dance music or meditation tunes. Songs that you know all the lyrics to will distract your thoughts. Play songs by female artists whose lyrics reflect being large and in charge.

You may have heard that dating right away should be avoided; that's a misconception. You should definitely actively seek dating opportunities as soon as possible. This new person may not be your next soulmate, but their constant attention will give you the jolt you need to stabilize your self-esteem.

Most relationships are bonded by some form of vulnerable intimacy. This can be sharing secret experiences taken to the grave by both of you, near death experiences, or sex. In both, chemical bonding occurs and is only broken after months of not seeing or smelling that other person. (Quite animalistic, but very accurate). Even if you're determined to remain single, the energy between you will exist until it dies out entirely. During that time, you must understand that you can't speed up time no matter what. So be around other people, keep busy, and trust that this will pass.

Sometimes, you have to change environments to help you heal. You might have to leave town and shift perspectives a bit. You can go away to a paradise somewhere. Just remember: do not call or send drunk texts. It always feels like the right thing to do, but rest assured, it breeds regret.

Another new environment could be somewhere nearby where the less fortunate dwell. Seeing beauty can relax your mind, but seeing extreme poverty, sick animals, or children can snap you into reality by providing context.

"I'd get really stressed out as an adolescent. I didn't know the word for anxiety, but it haunted me. One day, I was standing outside under a moonlit sky. That moon was so huge that night. I guess it was a Harvest Moon. I saw multiple shooting stars back to back, and in that moment, I felt so tiny compared to the grandness of the universe. Suddenly, my worries felt super small; recognizing that my problems were insignificant to the planet made me feel larger than life!"

— Journal Entry, 2009

The world has so much pain; just because yours exists doesn't mean it is worse than someone else's. Remember to be nice to people you come into contact with. Taking your low vibration out on someone will cause you to feel terrible later. It's also important to note that you don't have to endure their advice when spending time with loved ones or strangers. Be courteous to yourself by asking that person to talk about something else or excuse yourself from their presence. It's hard to delete toxicity, so it's better to flee! Isolation is your worst enemy during this breakup time. You'll want to lay on the floor crying for two months, so don't be lazy. Get up, get out, and force yourself to live life! You got this!

iii. [Be]come Poppin'

The many stages of grieving loss usually suck, but the Third Rule stimulates the excitement in your life and potentially changes the fate of your breakup. Glowing up is the process of upgrading various aspects of your life. To Become Poppin' is to redefine or exaggerate some part of yourself.

Get your hair done, a new outfit, pretty makeup, and/or that dental work you've always wanted. Enhancing parts of yourself will boost your self-esteem, and your ex may even become jealous (that could be good or bad)! Become a star for the night, dress up and look stunning, and allow yourself to soak up some healthy attention. Party like a Rockstar, but avoid destabilizing drugs. Drugs will be fun and exhilarating during the interim short while, but once your buzz hits a low point, you will be in a far worse state! Doing constructive turn-up activities is essential, even if that means only going out in the daytime. This segment of your breakup may include reckless behavior, so only be around non-judgmental friends, and don't post anything you'll regret on social media. Hot photos showing you having fun are okay, though!

Another part of your glow-up should include removing photos of your ex. Even if you think you'll reconcile in the future, at least hand over the files to your friend for safekeeping so you lose access! Welcome to single life! Although jumping right into dating helps you recover, remember that dating during this time is to keep yourself distracted and on point! Keep those legs shaved, and always be ready for action. This emphasis on feminine upkeep and remaining desirable keeps you out of the depths of breakup despair.

You will be reminded of your ex by comparing him to your Tinder date or the memes you see. It's okay to miss him; it's okay to cry. Redecorate your living space as a part of the glow-up. The more visible changes you see, the better you will feel, as long as they are positive alterations. You've heard that people lose the most weight when going through a breakup, and it's usually mentioned in a positive light. Working out is a great way to exert negative energy and feel a positive release. If you are going to lose weight from the breakup, please let it be from cardio and a healthy diet. Choosing to abstain from food or choosing to over-eat can have tremendously foul effects on your attitude. So much of your mood is dictated by body chemistry. Maintaining a healthy chemistry will make you think clearer and feel better. If you do the opposite, you will be in an endless crabby mood. Take care of your nutrition (Specifics in the Health Beauty and Wellness chapter)!

By glowing up, you place yourself in the driver's seat of your life, and being in a better mental space makes you more attractive. Perhaps the relationship is over for good. Sometimes, it takes a person 90 days to miss you and reassess their decision. If you are a hot mess, you'll ruin your chance. When someone decides they want to live without you, it's like a death—but it can really help you discover yourself.

Give it some time, and you may enjoy being on your own. Perhaps the person will try to come back; maybe not. But know that you have become stronger with more experience: Your next adventure will require all you have learned. You've glowed up, and you will love you for it!

iv. Bounc[ing] Back

Once you reach the stage of "I wish I never met him" vs "I want to be with him" stage, you're at a crossroads. A princess who respects herself rescues herself. You've felt like crap, and now it's time to make a big girl decision. Bounce back to your empowered self.

You respect yourself by deciding if you can survive without that ex of yours. If that answer is 'no,' you can take steps to pursue them further and lure them back to you. If the answer is 'yes, I can move on,' then own everything that happened, including the embarrassing parts of the breakup, and be on to the next. The world population is 7.55 billion, and 3.8 billion are male.

To lure a man back, it's best to do this visually. Get creative here. What do you know about him that you can incorporate into a surprise? Translate a poem into his native tongue. Create a video of you dolled up, describing your shared great memories. Whatever you record or send, keep it under a minute! If he has you blocked, have your friend send it to him. Only do this once, otherwise, it's considered stalking!

The key is to do the least talking possible and be ready with actions instead.

Show that you are serious about change. Angry? Enroll in anger management classes and send a photo of what you've learned from the pamphlet. Be truly vested in yourself, allow others to notice that, and roll the dice for the outcome. If 90 days have passed, it may be time to move on. If your friends are bashing him, politely ask them to stop since this doesn't help! Set a goal for yourself and focus on achieving it. Each time you level up, you will distance yourself from the breakup and increase your self-worth.

The pain decreases with the passing days as long as you can genuinely acknowledge what occurred. If you find yourself replaying scenes wherein you wished you had or hadn't said something, take a deep breath and say, "I forgive myself for XYZ. I forgive them for XYZ." The release will be tremendous! Remember, if you smell them or hear their voice, you will start the healing process again. Keep your distance, protect your energy, and bounce back!

Talk kindly to yourself. Write a gratitude list of ten things you are grateful for. Your power is in your womb. Place your hand onto your pelvis and breathe. Feel the body move up and down as you rest there. This is where life forms. You are powerful.

The breakup is something so commonly experienced; everyone has their own version of bouncing back into full recovery. Trust the process, lean on your friends for support, or place yourself in a new environment to make new friends!

In cases where you have dark thoughts regularly and don't feel safe, please get in touch with a suicide prevention hotline. They offer 24/7 support by listening to you, offering remedies, and helping you to see the big picture. You can even hire a therapist. Many online and affordable options provide financial aid, like Betterhelp.com.

Therapy doesn't mean something is wrong with you. It's like essential maintenance; nails, hair, and taking regular showers fall in the same category. A life coach will guide you in an unbiased way toward your future.

Grief hits people differently, and the loss of a relationship can be heavy. Comparing this to the death of someone close to you is pretty extreme, mainly because there is the absolute loss in death. Relationships still allow for hope for potential reconciliation.

"When my brother committed suicide, I never thought I'd be able to be happy ever again without that coming up. It's not something that defines my life anymore because I learned to give a safe space to that difficult thing. Once in a while, you go there, and it hurts really bad, but then you leave it there and can revisit it anytime. It's how humans are designed that we are resilient. I have faith and trust in the process. It will come for sure. It hurts so bad because

you couldn't prevent it. Eventually, I will get there, or everyone will contemplate ending their lives...things must work out eventually, right?"

–Roger

Remember, you were a beautiful growing person from the moment you were born. You will continue to grow through and beyond the experience. Forgive yourself for the decisions you made, forgive them for not being the long-term match for you.

"Things will get worse before they get better, but they always get better."

— Wendy

Anything you give your strength to or draw from is considered idolatry. Think about that. When you give your all to a relationship, your thoughts are bombarded, and the ups and downs dictate your life's ebb and flow. How much better to have your ebb and flow influenced by infinite love and wisdom than the inevitable unpredictability of life on earth. This book reveals, bit by bit, that the key to success in all domains is connecting one's subconscious and conscious mind to the spiritual realm where power and freedom operate.

QUADRANT 2

Spirituality

≈

Arguably the most important quadrant that sets the tone for all other areas of your life performance. The skeletal system holds things in place but what actually gets you moving and grooving is the entity inside of your body.

9. Aliveness

Spirituality *exists*, whether a person is aware or not. You are not your body. You exist in your body, along with your thoughts and emotions, which are also not you. So, who are *you*?

Quantum physics studies matter and energy at the most fundamental level. Quantum discoveries have been incorporated into the general population's chemistry, biology, materials, and astronomy knowledge. This summarizes life as you know it and draws attention to the energies existing within objects, like "you" who exists within your body.

Quantum science attempts to reveal how everything in multiple universes is connected to everything else via dimensions your senses cannot comprehend. There are many astonishing discoveries resulting from Quantum experiments, like the fact that the act of observation or measurement itself changes the outcome of an experiment.

Another cool thing is the phenomenon of Entanglement, wherein two or more objects are connected even when far apart, so they can be considered a single system. In Entanglement, information about one thing reveals something about the other, and the state of one relies on information from the other for a complete description.

Think of "twin-sense," where identical twins are said to feel what their sibling feels, or the widowhood effect, a phenomenon in which the loss of a spouse leads to the living widow dying themselves, usually within the following three months.

Your awareness of the spiritual realm is a huge yet primary first step towards living a life of empowerment and freedom. If you've lived ignorant of your true identity, that's okay because the wool has now been removed from your eyes, and a blissful existence awaits you!

To deepen your awareness, you can partake in various exercises. One such activity is to place your hand on your abdomen and take long breaths that fill your lungs to capacity and completely expel that air. This slows everything down. Observe your toes. Feel your feet and identify the points of contact; are your heels pressed into the floor, or are you balancing on the ball of your foot? Spend time observing your body working for you, the skin resting on your bones, housing your blood vessels. Many mechanisms are occurring around the clock to keep your body operating.

Despite all that occurs for your foot to remain responsive, you are not your foot; you have a foot. As you breathe, you observe that foot, and then you examine other body parts. What is your tongue doing? Feel the weight of your tongue resting in your mouth, perhaps resting against your teeth and cheeks.

While breathing, bring awareness to how much work your tongue does on a moment-to-moment basis, even without you chewing, drinking, speaking, or laughing. It is ready and able, waiting to be commanded, and filled with energy. Do you credit all of this to your brain? Head over to the brain for this discussion.

10. Turning Off Your Thoughts

Some actions require conscious thinking, while others, like breathing, are still functions of brain activity but don't require active thought. Have you ever turned off your thoughts and experienced absolute silence in your mind for a few seconds at a time? This critical exercise allows you access to other neglected parts of yourself, which generally take a backseat to your dominant thought habits.

You are not your thoughts; you have thoughts, but they are supposed to be your employees, not the boss. Your thoughts should work for you to accomplish problem-solving, enjoy pleasant memories, and other tasks you assign them to complete. If you constantly think and never experience complete silence and unadulterated existence, your thoughts rule you by taking up space and snuffing out your spiritual self.

Some scientists postulate that a person produces more than 6,000 thoughts daily, many of which are rumination (repeatedly going over the same thought). It helps to write down your thoughts so they have a landing spot that allows you to move on. This points to the popularity of journaling and is just one of many methods used to cease incessant thinking.

In some cases, you should seek the guidance of a therapist to assist you, but the point in bringing this up is to tell you that thoughts will go nonstop if you do not command the space. Don't fret, a lot of people think incessantly, just like you. The next time you catch yourself doing so, observe the thoughts as they pass by and refrain from making any judgments about them.

Perhaps your thoughts have rendered you successful in life, but do they have their limitations? In some cases, an ability to feel and sense will get you much further than any thought dissection can. Much of life is observation and deduction, but how exhausting and limited that is compared to simply grounding oneself and feeling which action to take.

You'd be surprised how practical intuition is; it is a tool to be strengthened through practice. In a decision as simple as, "Should I go to the grocery store," you can run down a bunch of reasons why you should go now versus later. You may look at your agenda's list to determine the order of operations, or you can take a deep breath, close your eyes, and feel the day's light pressing against your eyelids for a few moments. Much of thinking is focused on the past or the future, but being present in the now is where real life exists.

With your eyes still closed, feel your feet grounding down into the floor (even better if you are shoeless and can feel the earth outside like sand, grass, or soil. After resting there with a few deep and conscious breaths, open your eyes and let your answer be there. There are more in-depth explanations and methods of breathwork. This brief overview will familiarize you with your perhaps often-ignored inner being.

Once your decision emerges from that exercise, deliberately expect positive outcomes to result from it. Grow excited about your intuitive process. Shriek and reach upwards towards the sky with fingers outstretched and spread wide. Smile.

Anticipate the significance of whichever micro details emerge from this awaiting experience. As you act on that decision, take special care to observe everything that happens. Eye contact, the cracks on the sidewalk, the other vehicles passing by. All of these things are significant and play their part in communicating with you.

When you listen to a symphony arrangement, each sound contributes to the orchestra's performance. Your life is the same way. When you zoom through getting tasks done, or even slowly experience the drawl of your existence, you're not capturing the essence of what it means to be alive unless you're deliberate about it. Be intentional about being in the present moment, grab life by the reigns, and give it a ride. Do this for you, but also know that your energetic contribution affects your neighbor's experience.

11. Your Aura Either Attracts or Repels

≈

What is an aura? Have you ever been near someone and could tell that they were in a great mood, or even a sour one?

Much of communication is non-verbal, in gestures and other such body language, but some of that non-verbal communication is transmitted spiritually. Although you can't always see auras, they are the spiritual energy surrounding all living things.

This section on *Spirituality* will often reference the Hebrew/Christian Bible and some famous prophets, disciples, and saints. If you disagree with religion, don't let that deter you from absorbing the beautiful gems of information woven throughout these sections. The various concepts mentioned here happen to be exemplified perfectly in the Bible but are also supported in nature and other texts.

"As a result, people brought the sick into the streets and laid them on beds and mats so that at least Peter's shadow might fall on some of them as he passed by."

Acts 5:15 NIV

The influence of a person's shadow, energy, breath, ambiance, or vibe is enough to suck the air out of the room in a negative way or fill a lonely heart with love and healing abundantly. Imagine that feeling when you curl up on the lap of someone you feel safe and nurtured with.

Auras are typically felt, although it is also possible to see aura colors, with each color attributed to various characteristics. Whatever spirit is dominant in you, its features will proceed outwardly.

"Think happy thoughts, then they will pour out of your face as sunbeams, and you will always look pretty."

–Unknown

12. Your Dominant Spirit

~~~

Yes, the next few paragraphs are going to talk about Jesus Christ, so buckle up!

If you are the spirit inhabiting your body, what is the above reference to the dominant spirit? Is there more than one inhabiting your body? For Christians who have accepted Jesus Christ as their Lord and Savior, the Holy Spirit lives inside their body.

This is the Spirit of God that prompts you to take action, guides you on your journey, and reminds you that God is with you. It also chastises you when you are 'outta pocket' (in other words, participating in harmful nonsense). The Holy Spirit has characteristics detailed in the Bible called the Fruit of the Spirit: Love, joy, peace, goodness, meekness, gentleness, long-suffering, faith, and self-control (I Cor 10:3).

You can deduce what is inside a person based on their outward conduct, speech, and what aura they emit. Acting and hiding may get you far, but your true essence will eventually seep through your pores, so doing some spiritual housekeeping is imperative.

You want your inner being to be characterized by love, forgiveness, and more love because God is Love and everyone needs more of it!

Have you ever met someone who had too much love? If you sprinkle a little more of yours on top, they won't explode, they will maybe burst into contagious laughter and bliss.

"When I moved to British Columbia I met a vast community of East Indians for the first time. One in particular became my heartbeat. I presented tenants of my Christian faith to him, while he taught me about his Sikh religion. He explained that they believed all God's are one, thus they respect all religions. I explained my belief that unless Christ is acknowledged as the one true God, that he would be missing the point.

I must say, accepting his viewpoint helped me reconcile some of the condemnation I experienced throughout my life. By seeing that all religions had validity, I felt like I had a hall pass to participate in behaviors that were not acceptable in my religion.

He converted to Christianity. Not because I made him, but he said multiple people had approached him and explained that Christ was calling for him.

When I met him, I felt Christ was calling for him too, and I don't feel that way about everyone I meet. He maintained his belief in his God, while also accepting that Jesus Christ was now a bigger part of his life too.

I didn't think it was possible to keep believing in your own God, while also believing in Christ. There's a scripture that speaks to serving two masters, and how it's not possible because what happens when they clash?

From that experience I learned a few things: I don't have all the answers about religion. Jesus Christ is a person who we can communicate with and feel his presence. Relationship with Christ is more important that religiosity.

Other religious influences will actually alter your personal beliefs if you allow them to. I'm not certain that's a bad thing, but I do know that I started backsliding on some of my religious practices which ultimately made me feel like 'ick'.

I feel much more well-rounded as a person and as a believer after my encounter with my Indian friend. Converting to Christianity doesn't look the same for everyone. It was important for me to know where I stand and how I feel about my beliefs, and less about me trying to teach somebody else."

— *Journal Entry, 2023*

One of the greatest deceptions for a Christian is a divergence from Christianity towards spirituality. If you can keep up your same level of studying, worshipping and practicing the principles of faith, then exploring other belief systems is safe. But if you are abandoning your successful habits to adopt the unknown, you risk falling off the wagon. Sometimes going down a different path may be necessary to get a firm understanding of where you stand in your belief.

It's such a bumpy road that it is advised not to go that route! If you do, it is recommended to have a Christian accountability partner who you are honest with in telling them you are going to explore a new religion. That way, they can observe your changes and give you helpful feedback. You can determine if those changes are what you want for yourself or not.

If you are not a principled Christian and find yourself really wanting stability and consistent joy, you can make it unto the right path by studying the Christian bible which inspires behavior modification. (Start in Proverbs and Psalms).

Life just happens sometimes. Christ is a person who understands you better than you do, and he's with you every step of the way, even when that way is wayward.

His story is one that compels people to experience overwhelming gratitude. A story that makes people feel close to him.

He was a baby birthed by a virgin, who grew up spreading love and knowledge. He is God's son, a manifestation of God in human form. He felt pain, just as you do, experienced love and joy, but also suffering. He was ultimately publicly humiliated and eventually killed for professing that he was the Son of God. The story is multilayered as to why, some say jealousy and a battle for power led to this. While divinely, this was a part of God's plan:

To have a man who had no sin, die as a sacrifice for a sinful mankind. This needed to take place because God had expectations for humans, that were not kept. But what kind of God would he be if he didn't honor his own rules? Sinners could not enter into the kingdom of heaven, but by this sacrifice, could be granted a cleansing of their sins.

Isaiah 1:18 says, *"Come now, let us settle the matter,"* says *the LORD. "Though your sins are like scarlet, they shall be as white as snow; though they are red as crimson, they shall be like wool."* Which is basically how you are forgiven, in modern times, on a daily basis for your own sins.

'Passion of the Christ," directed by Mel Gibson, is an excellent portrayal that captures the crucifixion of Christ. It conveys the emotions shared by Christians all over the world, including the joy when Christ was resurrected and ascended into heaven.

There are some false doctrines out there, and some examples of Christians whose flawed behavior can lead to ridicule of the church. Skip all of that and explore who Christ is as a person! The bible books were divinely inspired by God and transcribed by common people, but it is believed that the divinity surpasses the fact that people wrote it. Someone has to do the Lord's work, right?

Read the bible books of Matthew and Luke, when Jesus walked the earth and learn how he navigated conversations and situations. How he showed compassion, but also rebuke. How he relied on God's words to battle evil, how his faith healed and instilled robust belief in random people.

People want power. Power comes in many forms, seduction being a big one. It's all good while it's good, but destruction is often delayed. Or sometimes destruction is like a thorn that slightly aggravates over a long period of time. You get accustomed to the feeling and carryon. It is possible to live without that aggravation, but it requires sacrifice to the way you're used to living.

The rise in numbers of people who abandon religion and do whatever they feel, can be attributed to wanting the power and not the sacrifice of obedience. Would you do it if you knew you could emit seductive energy to manipulate circumstances in your favor? The devil (Ruler of Darkness) is clever and may not openly suggest a person should become a witch to practice evil. Instead, he will encourage you to pray with crystals and burn sage. As time goes on, you are tossed in the wind and have a hard time deciphering which way is up.

There are so many videos online now of people who have lived a fast life, and then get baptized and have a completely different perspective. They often talk about feeling free and light, as a result.

How could the things you desire most be evil, if you've coveted them for such a long time! After all, God made you so if he didn't want you to have those desires, then why are they in you? You picking up a bible one day is not going to change you completely.

However, the bible is a transformative tool, and if you keep at it, your mind and desires will start to change on a spiritual level first, then your flesh will follow.

This book has bible verses sprinkled throughout, but it's important to provide Ephesians chapter 4 verses 1 through 16 to help summarize and contextualize some of what was stated in this chapter. Ephesians was transcribed by an Apostle named Paul who spread the teachings of Jesus in the first century world while imprisoned. Enjoy this minute long read, but if you must, skip ahead. Also, even if you can't interpret all of its meaning, your spirit is certainly absorbing it, which has reverberating benefits.

*Ephesians Chapter 4, New International Version
Translation:*

*"As a prisoner for the Lord, then, I urge you to live a life
worthy of the calling you have received. 2Be completely
humble and gentle; be patient, bearing with one another in
love. 3Make every effort to keep the unity of the Spirit
through the bond of peace. 4There is one body and one
Spirit, just as you were called to one hope when you were
called; 5one Lord, one faith, one baptism; 6one God and
Father of all, who is over all and through all and in all.*

*7But to each one of us grace has been given as Christ
apportioned it. 8This is why it says:*

*"When he ascended on high, he took many captives and
gave gifts to his people." b*

*9(What does "he ascended" mean except that he also
descended to the lower, earthly regions c ? 10He who
descended is the very one who ascended higher than all the
heavens, in order to fill the whole universe.) 11So Christ
himself gave the apostles, the prophets, the evangelists, the
pastors and teachers, 12to equip his people for works of
service, so that the body of Christ may be built up 13until*

*we all reach unity in the faith and in the knowledge of the
Son of God and become mature, attaining to the whole
measure of the fullness of Christ.*

*14Then we will no longer be infants, tossed back and forth
by the waves, and blown here and there by every wind of
teaching and by the cunning and craftiness of people in
their deceitful scheming. 15Instead, speaking the truth in
love, we will grow to become in every respect the mature
body of him who is the head, that is, Christ. 16From him
the whole body, joined and held together by every
supporting ligament, grows and builds itself up in love, as
each part does its work.*

Whatever your religious beliefs are, and even if you have
none, it's essential to identify which spirit is operating in you
at any given time. You can discipline your thoughts, but
without a spiritual self-awareness and awareness of
spirituality in the world around you, you'll be pulled in a
direction and wonder why you can't accomplish sustainable
change.

Who will be dragged down if you are around people with
different morals than yourself? Inquire, explore, and seek to
become clear about what you believe and then take it
seriously.

If you desire to be a Buddhist, immerse yourself and study to find out exactly how to be successful as a Buddhist. If you're a Christian, learn about who God says you are so you can own that identity. In moments of weakness, rely on your foundational teachings to power you through challenges with wisdom and the gift of discernment.

Now, remember there is no condemnation in Christ, so if you are a Christian who just read that section and feel a bit burdened to change your conduct, let that feeling of burden fall off you and to the floor.

This is just a little dose of medicine to wake you to the knowledge of what you already know.

If you are not a Christian and this all sounds so foreign to you, let it be a walkway leading you to explore more about the faith. You don't have to have it all figured out right now, this is just one tiny little seed planted, and God will lead you to various waters for it to grow.

If this is your bridge, you may confess with your lips that Jesus Christ is Lord and that you want to submit your life to pursuing his values and teachings. That is all it takes for you to convert.

Living a life devoted to Christ will affect your speech, thoughts and actions. While not all Christians devote themselves, it is a starting place for a beautiful journey.

You may have read all of this and decided it seems a bit delusional. Sometimes you have to start with your imagination and constructed reality to get you moving. *God is actually real,* so this leap of faith reaps phenomenal rewards! Inviting Christ into your life is major! Good luck! You got this! Now, moving right along to the next section.

13. Who You Are vs Who You Want to Be

❧

How do you achieve peace within yourself? Let's say you're harmonized internally with positive thoughts flowing, moments of silence where no thoughts pass by, only sounds of the environment and your breath. Everything on the exterior flows nicely with tremendous progress, and you feel good.

Anxiety rears its ugly little head occasionally due to a subtle comparison of your life to the life you wish you had. Anytime you don't have the tools or willpower to achieve something, it leaves you susceptible to feelings of inadequacy and low self-worth, thus internal chaos instead of peace.

"I wish you saw yourself the way I see you. You're beyond any blemish, acne, or anything you think is wrong with you. You don't own yourself. I'm dating this girl, and she fully owns herself. She's completely unapologetic for all aspects of her being and body.

–Do you think I'll ever fully own myself like her?

–No, because she is fully defined and operates from that position, you constantly self-examine and input new data. You're consistently evolving your being. Just like me, I do that too."

–a discussion with Dr. Hays

It's tough to acknowledge that you may lack certain attributes, even if your other qualities are fantastic. It's kind of like the saying, "My grandmother thinks I'm pretty." Yes, Grandma says it, but what about the people who aren't obligated to sugarcoat things?

You may appreciate that you are always adding new info and evolving (a defining characteristic), but perhaps you would also like to benefit from owning yourself, thus exuding unapologetic confidence like that woman Dr. Hays described.

Having someone like Dr. Hays pouring into you is a blessing because it's comforting knowing that someone you hold in high regard considers you perfect, flaws and all. Also, knowing that they share your traits is validating; social connections are how you relate to the world.

In the event you don't yet have that person to pump up your self-esteem, seek the support through positive affirmations you can find online.

Don't let the power of positive affirmations slip right by you, they are truly gems hidden in plain sight! Hearing and repeating affirmations that speak life into you is extremely powerful.

It's super important to feel like you are perfect as is, but it is also great to concurrently be aspirational. Go ahead and pursue more wonderful attributes. Take bits and pieces of admirable traits you observe in others and put together your best self, one who is accustomed to getting the results you want.

You don't have to detest parts of yourself just because you want to adopt new traits. Loving yourself is very important so you don't slide the slippery slope of envy. If you're shy but desire to be outgoing, first appreciate that shy people have the upper hand in observing before acting. The boisterous one risks saying things they'll regret later because they are so quick to speak.

"I thought I was introverted until I realized I am just an introvert around people who don't promote my peace. I enjoy being such an extrovert around people filling my tank!"

— *Journal Entry, 2023*

Cherish your shyness, be thankful you were forged that way, and advance toward a new world of extroversion! A deeper understanding of yourself as a limitless spiritual entity will release you from the limits you place on yourself.

14. You Are Not Your Emotions

You were created uniquely in the purest form, and in the image of God thus, you are love.

"How come you're so lovable? Because you are loved. Love loves. When you are in love, you have only a desire to love. You demonstrate who and what you are."

—Dr. Hays

If those statements are true, why do people sometimes act out of character? Negative emotions are normalized in society. People will convince you that bad feelings are natural and warranted in response to specific actions. It's the greatest lie ever told!

Are you a pre-programmed robot or a living, breathing being of free will with a throne awaiting you in heaven! You don't have to be inhabited by those negative emotions.

Pastor Willie Johnson introduced the concept of emotions as entities. When something occurs, do you feel yourself becoming angry or sad? Then that's an indication something is coming *at* you as opposed to already *being* you. Stop those emotions at the door and tell them, "No! This is my body. You can't come in." They *will* stop.

You have the authority to rebuke negative emotions as soon as they rear their ugly heads. With practice, you will experience shorter invasions of emotion, eventually remaining in a state of homeostasis and not being pulled in any direction without your permission. You will choose which emotions you wish to welcome in and also be in control of when they must leave. Stoics practice a complete control of their emotions, and have a huge following of Stoicism.

Pastor Johnson explained negative emotions as invaders, with their end goal being to get you to kill yourself. They pimp you. Offering to help you with no strings attached, promising empowerment or consoling if you just let them be in control for a few minutes. Sadness is known for that.

Typically, something happens and sadness comes around empathizing with you and seducing you into letting it in. You feel alone, but now that sadness is there, you feel comfort. Meanwhile, it is whispering for depression and anger to enter the side door and window. Next thing you know, they are in your living room, and you are too afraid to ask them to go. They operate your body and have you do and say things that harm others and make a fool of yourself. They do not care about you or the destruction that's caused each time they come around, meanwhile on the outside looking in, people wonder what's wrong with you.

"It doesn't have to be like that. It's all a choice. That's YOUR body. You decide what inhabits you at any given moment. We, as humans, duplicate by birthing; how do they duplicate? If you saw emotions as spiritual entities, you would not be so lackadaisical in allowing them to inhabit your body.

Emotions duplicate by taking over our personalities, thoughts, habits, and character. They lead with persistent behavior, conditioning you to operate from a baseline that is not you but them.

Soon enough, they define your personality traits, thus dictating how successful you are at achieving the results you want out of life. The best way to counteract the bombardment of emotions that seek to control you is to be filled with the following four pillars of emotional health and healing:

1.Love Everybody

2.Forgive

3.Respect

4. & Be kind, starting with towards yourself."

—Pastor Willie Johnson

If you exercise those as a standard of thinking and a barometer of how you should be feeling, you will successfully operate as your true form (LOVE).

"The desires of my heart used to be self-generated, but now they are God-generated. My desires, I felt I had to protect at all costs. I was on a long leash, and I prefer it much shorter, helping me to acknowledge who is at the other end...
(What God replied: I'm glad you're back; let me tell you what I have in store for you)."

— Journal Entry, 2017

When someone does you wrong, emotion convinces you to offer retribution. The opposite of peace is war. What do you hope to gain from the war, and what are you willing to let it cost you? Don't be manipulated; peace requires capturing thoughts and emotions (II Cor 10:5) and making decisions that flee evil. A life of peace is better than a life of vengeance (Rom 12:19).

A purveyor is a person who sells or deals particular goods or promotes an idea or view. When you become a purveyor of peace, you'll begin to live a soft life (the opposite of a hard life, characterized by grinding things out to get results).

This type of peace-forward thinking is unconventional to the average person. The visions others have for your life will not match your own. Don't expect them to. Dream big and live unapologetically, without explanation. A huge part of being able to act peacefully is asking God for the desire and the tools to do so. Your faith can be tiny, and He will still honor it because His wisdom and grace reward those willing to seek, knock, and ask.

15. Emotional Strongholds

Big dreams don't allow for the long-term residence of bitterness, resentment, or any other negative emotions, but why do they often feel impossible to eliminate? These are called Strongholds. It is likely a stronghold if you constantly feel resentment from every direction or some other consistent emotion. If you go to many different places and keep encountering the same concept or behaviors, there' a stronghold.

According to the Oxford English Dictionary, a stronghold is "A place that has been fortified so as to protect it against attack; a particular cause or belief that is strongly upheld." Examining your own life, these are the places where you've become stubborn and feel entitled to believe something, whether it is factually substantiated or not. You may not know your stronghold until you ask God to reveal it. Strongholds are things that have become a part of your identity and influence your actions and perception. You may be controlled unknowingly.

The first step towards freedom is identifying your stronghold, and the second is tearing it down. Daniel 10:1-21 states, "For the weapons of our warfare are not of the flesh but have divine power to destroy strongholds. No weapon that is formed against you will prosper." Psalms 9:9 tells you, "The

Lord is a refuge for the oppressed, a stronghold in times of trouble." The only stronghold you should want is the Lord your God so you can run to him in times of trouble. Let him be a strongly upheld belief and a place of refuge fortified against attack.

More often than not, the strongholds that you have in your life do not give you strength. Although you might consciously run to them when in trouble, they are like succubus and mirror the acts of the flesh described in Galatians 5:19-22:

"Sexual immorality, impurity and debauchery, idolatry and witchcraft; hatred, discord, jealousy, fits of rage, selfish ambition, dissensions, factions, and envy; drunkenness, orgies, and the like."

Visualize running behind the boulder of bitterness, hoping it will protect you when, in reality, it's blocking your view and access to the fruit of the spirit: "Love, joy, peace, forbearance, kindness, goodness, faithfulness, gentleness and self-control..." (Galatians 5:22-23).

It's much better to abide under the shadow of the Almighty, praying with intention and the power given to us by our Lord, and watching things come to pass.

Now ask yourself, do you even have the desire to want your strongholds gone? They have often convinced you they're your friends. You rely on them, and they are very familiar. They know you well and know when to back off and when to approach. They know when you are "On your Godly hype," so they don't buck against your boundaries then. They will lie in wait and come knocking on your glass when the timing is right.

Even though, as mentioned before, strongholds can be inherited from generational curses, you've also inherited the knowledge of Christ, should you so choose. "Jesus has given us the keys to the kingdom of heaven, and whatever we bind on earth will be bound in heaven, and whatever we loose on earth will be loosed in heaven when we pray His name" (Matt 16:19). Decide to cast out your strongholds and experience a life free of chains.

Did you know that ambition can be a stronghold! Enthusiastic ambition is a driving force led by the ego and can be addictive; there's nothing like it. When you have a vision, you will execute it to the fullest because it's what you like, and you're going after it!

You're not sure if this concept of yielding to God can move you the way your addictions move you. Rest assured, every time you relent and go with what God is pulling you towards, you learn from those outcomes that He always has good, the best, perfect, and lacking nothing awaiting you.

Deny your emotions discourse; they are no longer driving the train. "Abide in [Christ] and [he abides] in you…" (John 15:4). The allure of the other tendencies begins to fade because God reveals to you: That's not where wisdom, truth, and love habitually reside. They are identified as counterfeit, promising you safety and freedom but repeatedly proving to be limited and limiting.

As He pours into you, you learn His thoughts, words, actions, habits, and thus character. You recognize His voice, so when the other voices attempt to lead you, you identify the author and denounce their instruction.

The most freeing aspect of spiritual fortitude and Christianity is coming to the knowledge of who you actually are. In this evolving landscape of personal identity, and social expectations, social media, it is easy to gleam insight into yourself through comparison and whatever is being promoted as "good," "bad," or "in." In "cancel culture," one wrong step could banish you to becoming an unpopular outcast. It sounds stressful.

Your true identity is irrespective of your confidences, shame, experiences, physical traits, thoughts, and feelings. Who you are inside as an energy source is a spirit who is described in the Christian bible as:

forever loved (Rom 8:38-39),

healed (Isai 53:5),

strong, (Psalm 18:32),

forgiven (1 John 2:12),

belonging to a great family (Eph 1:5),

whole (Col 2:10),

belonging to a powerful God (Isai 43:1),

hopeful (Jere 29:11),

purposeful (Esth 4:14),

victorious (1 Corin 15:57),

has direction (Is 30:21),

peace-filled (John 14:27),

filled with joy (John 15:11),

loved, powerful, and have a sound mind (II Timothy 1:7),

wonderfully made (Psa 139:14),

worth it (John 3:16).

The first step in tearing down strongholds is to familiarize yourself with your spiritual identity by reading about it in a sacred text like the bible.

The biggest weapon against depression and anxiety is knowing your true identity underneath your outside shell. Any imagination that contradicts what you know is true about yourself will be cast down and kicked out. Makes it so much easier to navigate through life when you protect your mind and heart with truth.

The next step is to fully immerse yourself into studying about it. When and if you decide to practice, you will reap the full benefits instead of half-stepping and then complaining about how religiosity and spirituality are a sham. You can ask for like-minded individuals to be drawn closer to you so you can build a network of people who can lead and inspire you to delve deeper into your interests. But who do you ask?

16. Prayer vs Manifestation

∾

Praying for an outcome and manifesting are similar concepts, whereas the latter relies on positive vibes to fuel your request, while praying requires asking the Creator. Both require specific intentions and faith.

If you ask for "things to go your way," you may get marginal results, but if you ask to be "hired for a new job and it to teach you how to become a great leader," you are narrowing your focus, improving the accuracy of your aim, thus more likely to see results which speak to your request.

Faith is believing in things that are not yet seen. The sooner you exercise faith about a request, the more reward you get. The vibrations within and around you seem to awaken the surroundings, and everything in your environment will communicate to you. You'll ask about a job, believe you'll receive that job, and suddenly see commercials about that industry or meet someone in a grocery store who is the recruiter for that company.

It's incredible how alive things are even without people paying attention; when they tap in, the magnanimous sensation of being interconnected flows effortlessly and surrounds them. If this is something you've experienced yourself, then this description resonates, and if you're new to it, tremendous thrills await!

You may have said some form of prayer for many years but have never prayed. Now, this next section will remind you of 5 steps for how to pray powerfully:

17. How to Pray Powerfully

i. You must have something specific to pray for. Falling to your knees with no action of the heart is like a woman who goes to the store and doesn't have anything to buy (Pastor Charles Spurgeon). She may end up with some purchases, but how better to have self-examined and prepared her soul with her true needs. When you request a meeting with a Queen or King, you must come as close as possible to a plan to not waste time or make a fool of yourself. God is a King, so come prepared.

ii. The key to petitioning in prayer is not moving on to the second thing until you have fully pleaded the first. You ramble many things at once, naming people, topics, and circumstances—so which specific thing should God hear?

iii. Do not convolute your message with eloquent words you don't fully grasp. Your prayer is measured not by its length or intelligence but by its honest divinity.

iv. If you know you have effectively pleaded your case, you would not emerge from prayer with doubt. If you have doubt, then you did not pray with your heart! You must believe it to be true that you communicated with the Almighty. You will be able to say, I now know he has heard me; thus, the outcome is undoubtedly his design!

If you're unsure which scriptures confirm that God will answer your prayers, do a Google search.

Dictionary.com defines a Decree as "An official order issued by legal authority." In Luke 10:19, Jesus tells us: "I have given you authority to trample on snakes and scorpions and to overcome all the power of the evil one; nothing will harm you." John 16:23 states, "...Whatsoever you shall ask the Father in my name, he will give it to you." This establishes the spiritual authority Christ gives you so you can make decrees.

v.   For those who wonder, "Why pray if I can't change what God has already planned?" When you pray, the Holy Spirit inspires your soul with what you should petition for. Thus, your prayer carries an omniscient characteristic.

The decree of Psalm 112:1, "I am blessed," establishes a blessing in your life, which separates you from anything that would come against it. It's also an example of how simple yet powerful your decrees can be. Be direct and ask God for precisely what you want; it will go forward as law. "You shall also decree a thing, and it will be done, and light will shine on your ways " (Job 22:28).

If this spiritual power is all new to you, it can seem mythical, mystical, and strange. The mind wants to be in control, but it's merely an instrument. Don't let it play you.

The mind's job is to hold onto and attach to things, and it's your job to choose which thoughts to keep. You are in control, but your powerful mind will convince you of the impossibility of pressing mute. As mentioned earlier, sitting in silence and observing the thoughts that pass through is an enlightening experience. You'll learn what your self-talk sounds like. But realize those thoughts are not you; you are the observer.

When you ask for the highest and best to come your way, you must take a leap and trust that whatever comes to you will be precisely that. You must trust that things are happening for you, not against you. Sometimes, the most challenging experiences teach the best lessons; embrace them all as a part of your journey.

Understand that we are in societies that move very fast. In the early 90s, you'd have to keep a pencil and pad next to the phone to write a message. It was nice if you missed the call, they would have to wait until the next day to reach you. Now, there is 24/7 availability and connectivity. You have to be the one to slow down to create moments of stillness. Here in that space, answers are revealed, where you are most powerful. It's a gift that takes only 5 mins, 2 mins, and one minute to breathe and be silent.

You are special and unique. Finding your purpose requires asking a lot of questions. Those questions are answered once you ask.

You will live through certain things, and your mindfulness will dictate how much you grow from them.

"You have to learn what sparks the light in you so that you, in your own way, can illuminate the world."

—Oprah

Life never stops teaching; once you've achieved harmony within yourself and overcome personal obstacles, your scope will widen, and you'll become more of a force in the world. You'll start impacting those around you by showing up, carrying yourself, and adding to things with your aura.

You'll be surprised to learn how valuable you are as soon as you start the internal work. Your path will take wonderful turns, and you'll finally enjoy the full meaning of life.

18. How To Elevate Your Emotional State

❧

People only accept, believe, and surrender to the thoughts equal to their emotional state. The best way to elevate your state is with gratitude. Did you know that over 1,000 chemical reactions restore and repair the human body when in appreciation?

It's tempting to turn to sex, food, drugs, work, and socializing. But with those things, you always come down from the elevation at some point. Can you quiet your thoughts? You have to be OK when things stop moving.

But how can I be grateful when everything around me sucks? The first step is to believe that you can immediately change what is sucking joy from you. How? Altering your external situation may be a process, but clearing the space in your mind and heart can be done immediately.

Remember, your mind is a tool. Thoughts come and go, but you are not your thoughts; with the help of meditation, hiring a therapist, or listening to affirmations, you will have them under control. Write down a timeline of events to provide an accurate picture of what your life is really like. You may think you are a victim when the facts say otherwise.

To adjust your emotional state and thus reality, you must take accountability for life you've already created. Some of the decisions you made or did not make placed you in your situation. Let this be an empowering fact, not a depressing one because the power to make different decisions rests in your hands. Take a moment and give thanks for the ability to make other decisions, to change whatever sucks for you.

Change your narrative, and fabricate a new story until it becomes true! Your mental health consists of the thoughts that repeat in your head, your recounting of events, and how you talk about yourself to others. I'm lucky to be alive! My future is bright! I deserve the greatness that is coming my way!

Share your faith with only people who will offer unabashed support and celebration. Don't waste your time discussing your heart's contents and dreams with Negative Nancy's, Debbie Downers, and "Realists."

> *"How do you expect land rodents and chickens to understand the flight path of an eagle?"*

> **—–Dr. Dewaina R. Hardee**

Setting boundaries to protect yourself may be challenging, and people may become upset, but you are always worth it. Your life will change once you're clear on what is non-negotiable for you, and act with this mind as often as you can. Practice asking for what you want and need!

To delve into your soul will require action beyond watching videos but actually doing the described work. Take a genuine first step.

You have to become clear about who you are, and can accomplish this by asking yourself a few questions. What do you desire? How do you want to be perceived? What must cease to exist for you to live your full self? Being solely a fear-inspired pleaser of others in pursuit of avoiding micro-rejections is much different from living your truth with every decision. You become an architect of your life by gaining clarity on who you are.

19. Vision Boards

Imagine putting a visual to the ideas you have in your head and being able to stare at that vision multiple times a day. That summarizes how a vision board works while skipping over some important details.

Vision boards are excellent because as you collect images of what you desire, those images are now actually a part of your environment--splashes of color, fast cars, and all. The poster board doesn't just sit on your wall; whatever is on there springs into your reality.

"Mom, what would you say about Vision Boards? I don't want readers to become distracted and try to shortcut by manifesting things that are wrong for them."

"I listen to the Word, I hear podcasts, I'm looking for the Lord in nature, these are my visions. I'm looking for Him (God) in every aspect of my life. It may be a color that inspires me to do something or the sun's rays. We are all spiritual beings; it's about who your God is. Whatever is speaking to you is shaping your environment and your desires. Culture is people, circumstances—external things. If you are into fitness, then culturally, you'll be interested

in nutrition and those kinds of things. Whatever you're about, your culture is going to speak to that. What are you watching, who are you watching, how are they promoting your goals? How are the podcasts and environment enriching you? If those things are not helping you reach the things you need to do, why are you doing them?"

— a discussion with Dr. Dewaina R. Hardee

While it's important to curate your environment, when too much of your focus rests on material things, disappointment and heartache await the fading façade. Take time to ask God what will better your existence, and you will naturally be drawn to those things that increase love and prosperity in your life.

It's like buying shoes precisely the size of your foot, which hurt as you walk around, versus getting a pair with some wiggle room. You can ask God for $10,000, or you can ask for the freedom and stress-free feeling of having $10,000; once you are made aware of the depths of your desires, you might improve the accuracy of what you're manifesting.

It's helpful to make multiple vision boards over time to see how your desires are refined from one board to the next. Some things may carry over because you are so happy with them, while others will be taken off entirely once you realize it wasn't all you thought it would be.

Take a moment to write or draw a picture of your new future; the universe will conspire to make your vision a reality. Manifestation is willing something into existence, focusing on it, and drawing it close to you until it becomes your experience.

You don't have to be religious to be able to manifest a life of your dreams. A perspective and spirit of expectant optimism powers your manifestation because you must visualize yourself already with what you want. It's the expectation and undeterred focus that brings it to fruition.

In the Christian bible, 1 John 3 verses 5 and 8 say, "You know that (Jesus) appeared to take away our sins"; "The son of God appeared for this purpose, to destroy the works of the devil." Translated into a few other versions, this reads that "Jesus was manifested." Why bring up the bible there? Well, manifestation gets you far in life; it works, and as your courage to ask for more increases, so does your bounty.

Sometimes, you'll manifest things you don't want or are unprepared to handle. Imagine manifesting a few million dollars but not having the wisdom to visualize yourself knowing what to do with the money.

Wisdom lets you picture a detailed larger picture, perhaps investing, delegating, hiring financial planners, and how your life will look with the new influx of cash. That money could shipwreck you and leave you with uncontrolled drug addiction, exposure to mentalities and lifestyles that harm your internal harmony, and who knows what else.

The Holy bible acknowledges that manifestation is real, as Jesus himself was manifested, as was his purpose. Manifestation is a powerful and necessary tool, but without the gift of wisdom that comes from studying the ancient scriptures, anything goes.

20. Love is the Main Event

~≈~

Love is the key to joy and self-actualization. Loving oneself, loving others, doing everything from a place of love, expecting love from others, being love itself. That may seem cliché or overly simple, but it's true.

"How do I know if what I'm doing is wrong? How can I reconcile this crazy fast lifestyle in Houston dancing and sugaring with what you say?"

"With every interaction, every thought, have love as your objective and orientation. Desire to give love to the men you meet it will never steer you wrong. It does not mean you will always receive love back. Still, guard your heart by being the gatekeeper of what and who enters it. Experience will teach you how to filter, but regardless, pouring into others with love is the key to remaining blemish-free and elevating your soul."

"Hmm, interesting; always have the intention of love. I got it."

–A discussion with RCH

Lisa Bevere, a New York Times Bestselling author, wrote (and not necessarily in this order), "Love cannot go deeper than the room the heart makes for it. As we obey truth, our hearts are refined to love one another deeply.

"A heart that resists truth can love only superficially. Outside of truth, love is impossible. When the Word has its way in us, we love and produce fruit that remains because it is holy and true. Abiding in God's Word increases our depth and capacity to truly love."

Once you get a taste of how magnetic the intent of love is in drawing beautiful experiences toward yourself, your direction for manifestation will take on a whole new shape and excitement. Love connects you to the human experience in ways you can't yet imagine, since you were created by love Himself (1 John 4:8 says, "God is love").

You were created with love, to be loved and to love. Love is your purpose, your destiny, and your power. Studying the intentions of who made you will give you powerful insight as to the things you should want, things that will in no way cause you harm.

"For I know the plans I have for you, declares the LORD, plans to prosper you and not to harm you, plans to give you hope and a future"

—Jeremiah 29:11 NIV

Renewing your mind is equivalent to clearing the cache on your computer, refreshing a web page browser, erasing a whiteboard, and giving yourself a great big stretch before taking your next step. Sure, you can go days, weeks, months without doing so and things will operate just fine. Imagine choosing to refresh more often, though, and the potential power therein!

"Do not conform to the pattern of this world, but be transformed by the renewing of your mind. Then you will be able to test and approve what God's will is—his good, pleasing, and perfect will."

—Romans 12:2 NIV

You can find knowledge of the highest will for your life, and become aligned with desiring and manifesting that version in love. The Lord says, "Then you will call on me and come and pray to me, and I will listen to you" (Jerem 29:12 NIV).

This renewing of the mind can be achieved in many ways. For Christians, it is through reading or listening to the ancient bible text; there's just something transformative about reading or listening to the truth that helps calibrate everything else for optimal existence! Did you know you can own an electronic device that literally plays only the bible? There's so much information and opportunities available.

Your lens in how you approach the world will be empowered and protected because the truth will permeate your deepest parts of self and lead you to specific paths of self-discovery. You spend efforts trying to figure out things that will be gifted to you almost magically once you spend some time reading the ancient words. Try it for yourself, start in Proverbs and Psalms, and read one chapter of each a day for 31 days. Watch what happens to you!

To recap the last few paragraphs, because let's be honest, all this spiritual talk can be pretty dense and maybe dull, but extremely pertinent:

A. Manifestation doesn't require love, but the wisdom to manifest what's best for your life does. Manifestation does require optimism and focus.

B. With love as your intentions and as a focal point of what you claim as a part of your identity, there is no limit to what you can create for yourself.

C. Your internal spiritual system predicates your exterior, thus all the other compartments of the bento box. It has the most significant influence because with everything else in place, and this one lacking, you'll always experience falling short of fulfillment. You may successfully capture experiences that feel potent and robust, but those are always fleeting.

D. When your feelings tell you you're hot, then you'll believe you're hot; If your senses tell you you're great, you'll think you're great, but the truth is you just are hot and great no matter what your fluctuating feelings communicate because God says so! The same mighty God who created the mountains, birds, laughter, and sunshine.

Your soul is a part of your vessel that goes through multiple experiences, whether you actively acknowledge its existence or not. If you nourish your soul in the right direction, there is no limit to what you may achieve.

When acting out of desperation, you face trials and tribulations that have the advantage over your mind, body, and soul. It's indicative that you are walking without consciousness and unaware of your true surroundings, dangers, and potential blessings.

When you seek God, everything in your environment becomes alive, and you'll decipher messages from nature that support you on your path of self-discovery. Some of what you discover may be difficult, as sometimes having a mirror reveal our shadows of the past calls us to live on a higher vibration requiring change.

Change can feel like death, but removing your shackles leads you to the life you want! Some people face themselves, do the work, and emerge victorious! Be that person.

There are so many communities of people just like you, making changes just like you, and sometimes failing, just like you. Start those conversations and clique up with each other for support. It's as simple as asking, "Hey what are your spiritual beliefs?" and letting the conversation take form from there. If that's too confrontational, you can ask, "Hey, how do you keep yourself balanced internally when you're having a bad day?" People are often relieved to speak about their internal processes.

Tapping into your truth keeps you anchored in peace, regardless of what's happening in the other sections of your bento box.

QUADRANT 3

Hygiene, Beauty, and Wellness

～

Looking, smelling, and tasting good allows a person to emit confidence that influences any environment. Beyond vanity, these are indicators of physical health and important pieces to your puzzle. Perfection is achieved when the minor details are tended to, which requires consistency and discipline. Is perfection attainable? Maybe not, but aiming as high as possible means all losses are high caliber.

21. Know Thyself

The most considerable receptors of data for humans are the 5 senses. Sight, touch, smell, sound, and taste. To get everything you want, you must present yourself as everything "they" want. You achieve this by constantly beautifying yourself for each sensory organ. Always look good. Always have skin that feels good. Always smell good and always taste good. Contributing your beauty to the world will produce grand returns.

As you learn yourself, you'll establish boundaries for your self-care regimens. Instead of letting your hygiene get out of hand where you are uncomfortable and feeling icky, you'll see the value in having a short tolerance for flaws. Right now, you already know yourself and how you like to look, but are you hard on yourself about it?

There's a difference between being disciplined and self-critical. When you're out, should you check yourself in the mirror occasionally? Totally! Few things are worse than realizing your tampon string was visible under your dress or a tiny green piece of spinach between your teeth. But learn to laugh at yourself for imperfections, knowing that you are on your way to having decreased amounts.

Go ahead and ask that question: but aren't looks genetic? Minimally, yes, but you can transform yourself into whatever is needed to achieve a goal. Deciding what type of look you want others to see you as is the first step in putting together the pieces to become her.

Although you're uniquely created in God's image, there's no need to reinvent the wheel when figuring out how you want to portray your physical self.

Are you a hot pink and glitter Barbie, a savage hood chick, a corporate boss, a soccer mom, or a punk rocker? Study other women who fit your ideal description, allow her to be your prototype, and download a mental picture of whichever 'program' she's operating from. This is often a cartoon character, actress, or other public figure, although sometimes it's someone you know personally.

What does her voice sound like? What is her range of wardrobe picks? Does she walk quickly or slow with a nice bounce to her butt? What's cool about people-watching is that you can observe someone candidly and notice all the subtle characteristics. When they eat, are they pouting their lips, wrapping them around the strawberry, or taking little nibbles? What are you gravitating towards? Then do that!

Practice by recording yourself for minutes at a time doing mundane tasks, and then review. What are your fidgeting behaviors? How many teeth show when you do a belly laugh? Do you like that? Whatever you don't love, train yourself to change.

If you watch reality shows renewed for subsequent seasons, you'll notice that each season touts improved makeup and hair looks. At the actors' cores, their personalities are consistent regarding behaviors and speech, but their appearances are always leaps and bounds away from the first season. Some would argue that their paychecks from the show allow for improvements, which is valid. But the main factor is self-awareness.

Seeing yourself on the outside is an essential tool often overlooked and taken for granted. A balancing act must occur between tending to your exterior but being grounded internally and not falling prey to pursuits of vanity—easier said than done; equally challenging is focusing your efforts and energy on internal prosperity while maintaining self-care of your exterior.

External maintenance allows you to remain functional in society and pleased upon looking in the mirror or smelling oneself. Acquiring a spiritual depth wherein the outside appearance is not the dictator of your self-love requires a journey. If you're all outside-based, a scarring accident could leave you feeling worthless, so it's super important to bolster your interior while not downplaying the outside!

When your self-esteem decreases due to some acne breakout, you share that experience with others worldwide, so don't worry! Just don't remain in that place; remember what you learned earlier: you are not your looks or your feelings. You are you. Those other attributes are accessories.

You can decide how you want to feel at any moment; that's your body! Tell that spirit of insecurity to GET OFF OF YOU!

"In sunny Beverly Hills, California, lunch with my hottie Russian Barbie friend Daria usually consisted of a salad and just enough water to wash it down; Intake resulting in a protruding tummy was out of the question. Our attire was usually a brightly colored, skin-tight dress or designer denim jeans and a crop top. Very little room for meal-time error.

The dining scene was perfect for practicing our mannerisms and conversation etiquette. We were on friend dates, each bite of food petite enough to hide in our mouths should we be approached and have to quickly shoot a sensual grin or witty reply. We sat up straight, usually at a table with high visibility, always seeking to absorb the attention upon anyone's arrival. We had a great time putting on a show, advertising our potential as perfect future girlfriends for eligible bachelors.

In Los Angeles, the car you ride matters. We noted who pulled up in which car: Rolls Royce's, G Wagons, Lamborghinis, Porches, Maserati's, and, of course,

Bentley's communicated much and quickly. We took a car service everywhere, and then when the night was over, I'd get a ride to my car to finish the 30-minute drive home myself. It was vital to be thin and beautiful in our world. Dinner was one thing, but the club was another.

Hollywood happened to people quickly. You'd arrive at 11:45pm on the red carpet at Supperclub and be whisked inside instantaneously by an assuming promoter who raised his eyebrows at you, pointed, and mouthed, "How many?" Either that or you were with a party with bottle service VIP entry, so telling the doorman their last name would suffice. Soon enough, she and I would be led to a table and asked what we wanted to drink. Alcohol has a high calorie count and even higher bloat risk, so only one bubbly drink would be the plan.

Rewind, so imagine that same red carpet with two scenarios that exemplify Hollywood happening fast:

Scenario A: You show up to a club, but the dress you chose is too tight, and you look uncomfortable and stressed. That dinner you ate the night before, and your barely there fat is bulging in the wrong places. The promoter points to your friend, mouths, "How many?" and when his eyes drift to you, the number two guest of the party, he looks down at his phone, and she receives a text. "No offense, but I can only get you in."

Scenario B: You and your friend arrive at the club, confidence on a million. You have a promoter connect to quickly get you in the door. You've forged a great connection because of your reputation for being dressed nicely, smelling good, and being a treat to have around. You lean in for a platonic kiss on both cheeks. At this point, your sweet fragrance fills his nose, and your soft voice fits the expectation very well. You and your friend skip the line. The night goes quickly because you won before the inside-the-club experience even started. You meet fun people and exchange numbers. Another fun night in Hollywood!"

— *Journal Entry, 2011*

22. Look Perfect

Wise people will warn that beauty fades with age, but hygiene is something you can always control. A man once said, "I want a girl whose sweat smells good, not masked with deodorants and cologne." This requires nutrition awareness. What you eat and drink directly determines your odor and taste.

How much time you set aside to prune yourself will directly correlate with the type of plant you blossom into. Once an impression is made, you may be unable to redo it. It's best to always be prepared. Ensure that your "Lazy-ugly-Day" still has a colorful head scarf to hide your messy hair, manicured nails to blow your snotty nose, and a practiced tone of voice to complement your flu-induced scratchy throat.

These things always matter. It is best to obligate yourself to a routine, becoming sensitive to slacking off. Keep being perfect until it becomes who you are on autopilot. Then, ideal situations will draw themselves to you.

Even an ugly girl can look perfect if she follows the rule of always looking perfect. Experimenting with which body butters and masks have the most remarkable effects, snacking on grapefruit, scrubbing with lemon, and taking photos of yourself in outfits to practice for going out are manageable steps.

An ugly girl can look more perfect than a pretty girl who isn't aware of the rule. The cute girl often relies on her natural looks, which makes her think she can coast through life, but there are levels to this. Being consistent and constantly upgrading makes you perfect. Powerfully magnetic energy is harnessed when you look perfect; this is the end goal.

Yes, the people you interact with are drawn by your impeccable hygiene and wardrobe, but what's behind those senses really hooks them in. The energy you exude when you know your body is prepared for all five senses is intoxicating and can influence people. It communicates, "Give me what I want. Do it now." Your subconscious mind sends a message to you that says, "I deserve this." That message is then broadcast to your body language confidently. You are in a relaxed emotional state, and every time you pass a mirror, you smile.

Smiles are contagious, and laughter is medicine. Look your best to feel your best. Think about a time when you judged someone by their appearance. Perhaps their sneakers were filthy, and none of their clothes matched. Now imagine that person having an angelic voice, even if they were hungry or mad. The importance of pursuing perfection of all the senses lies in our shortcomings.

There may be an emergency wherein you narrowly escaped a fire naked and had to cover up with clothes and shoes you found in an alley. Because you've trained to present yourself perfectly all the time, you have a default angelic voice, naturally smell like candy, your skin feels like Egyptian cotton, and your sweat tastes like salty pineapple. You look like a bum, but your lips are soft, and you would be the first pick in anything at that moment. Limitlessness is the goal!

"If you ever need to apply nail polish in a hurry, run your freshly painted toe under cold water for 30 seconds. It will be fully dry for you to walk out the door. Please, honey, never leave the house with wrinkled clothes. Look your best, always. You're so beautiful it should be fun!"

-Granny Ruth Standley

23. Hygiene

～

Hygiene and moisture are synonymous with beauty and health. The popular girls who helped to cover this topic are Russian, Black-American, German, Latina, Persian, African, Jamaican and Czech. Here's what they had to say about Hygiene:

If you have really intense body odor (BO) modify your diet by intaking pressed vegetable juice and increased water for two days —you'll immediately notice a difference. Your goal is to make even your sweaty moments smell good too; there are ways to mask BO but fragrance is an indicator of internal body chemistry and external bacteria, so get a head-start by refreshing from within.

Choose designer soaps that smell like high-end perfumes and body scrubs that carry the scent of fruit. When you wash yourself, give extra time to sweat prone areas and follow up with a granulated scrub using an exfoliating towel or glove. Scrubbing with baking soda does wonders in managing odor. Some Korean bath houses offer a useful service where they scour your full body. Commit to removing genital and pit hair, thus successfully ridding odor trapping epidermal layers.

Use panty liners to swap throughout your day, which is like putting on a new pair of panties. If your deodorant doesn't work, upgrade to one that does; make sure you add a thick layer, keep it close by in case you need a touch up, and don't be shy about choosing one for your genital area too.

You don't want an unexpected smell to assault any nostrils, especially when it's hot out or when hitting the gym. A general rule is if you can smell yourself assume everyone else can too. Sometimes it's not you it's your improperly washed clothes. Pre-soaking them in detergent makes a difference but you also need to know when to retire a garment. Keep a fresh emergency outfit in your trunk along with other essentials.

The girls especially wanted to draw attention to hair fragrance. A guy once said, "I love natural hair because it smells fruity, some of those weaves are stale." There is nothing wrong with either style just make sure it smells delicious when a breeze hits you.

Next on their list was great oral hygiene; if you're not brushing your tongue and flossing, your breath is likely subtly noxious because whatever you don't clean rots. While keeping gum and mints around is helpful, a healthy mouth doesn't compare.

Lastly, here's a special trick for helping your perfumes carry their longest enduring smell: First apply a base layer of lotion, spray your fragrance on top, then finally seal it with more lotion. You're welcome!

One of the girls participated in an experiment wherein vegetables and water were withheld for 12 hours, but odor masking techniques were applied, and by the end of the day poor BO prevailed. Then she maximized vegetable and water intake and did not add any deodorant or other remedies: her end result was no BO. The bottom line for smelling great is a healthy consumption of water and vegetables, the other tips and tricks are a bonus. Do what it takes to become your greatest YOU.

24. Moisture

The girls with supple skin have rigorous routines for applying lotions, oils, and serums. You don't have to break the bank to get high-end products, but you must be consistent with whatever you use. They agree that the first indicator of aging is dryness of the face, hands, and décolletage. Treat those areas with the same care you should give your look. Wear sunscreen under your makeup even if you don't think you need it because your sun exposure is secretly causing you damage. Use satin or silk pillowcases and sheets to protect the moisture in your skin and hair.

Your lips should be as soft as butter, so exfoliate them often and upgrade your chapstick or balm to a lip serum that repairs and provides ultimate moisture. Some lipsticks overly dry your lips, and a few of the girls prefer to apply a lipliner for the whole lip instead; it's less messy and lasts longer.

Occasional eye drops brighten the whites of your eyes but don't overuse them, or you'll create a dependence. For long hair, moisturize first with conditioner, then oil to seal. If you add oil to your hair first, you will inadvertently block the absorption of your conditioner. Stargazerhair.com has an excellent organic hair growth and hair health system to assist you.

Instead of treating moisture like an extra step, find ways to make it a staple of your beauty routine. If you use your hands to massage serums onto your face, rub any excess onto your palms and fingers. Some girls take it up a notch by moisturizing their hands and feet, then wearing plastic bags underneath gloves and socks to create a heat mask.

Another tip is to trade regular body wash and shaving creams for ones that exclaim moisture. Hyaluronic Acid is a molecule our bodies produce that binds water to our skin and joints, but this decreases with age. Do yourself a service by using products containing Hyaluronic Acid and Vitamin C. The girls suggest consuming multivitamins every night and Collagen, Biotin, and MSM, which support skin complexion, elasticity, and hair growth.

If you're too lazy to moisturize after a wash, take a leap of faith and do it once; apply oils to your whole body and observe how good you feel when one leg presses against another or when your hand strokes your forearm. Notice the niceness and understand that your skin screams for it.

The girls all agree that a consistent daily routine is imperative for sustained results. In the biblical book of Esther, candidates for marriage to the king first underwent 12 whole months of rigorous beauty treatments before even being introduced to him. That's a great indicator that beautification is a lifelong marathon, not a short race. To become a well-manicured woman, you'll need a plan, but a goal without steps is merely a dream.

25. Curated Settings

～

L ooking perfect requires you to have an excellent-looking environment as well. Whether in a penthouse or a place you don't like, put up pictures, hang pretty fabrics, and adjust the lighting. You deserve the illusion of perfection at all times because it's a mood enhancer. The beautiful things you are attracted to are also attracted to you. Gravitate those things towards you by:

A. Taking moments to appreciate subtle beauty in your environment.

B. Recording yourself so you can see how things look from another perspective.

There are a lot of hustle and bustle busy moments in life, but stopping to acknowledge an interesting cloud formation, a collection of pretty rocks, or someone's handwriting carved into the stump of a tree, all of those things are artful and the more you develop an eye to catch what's often all around you, you'll increase the frequency of their presence in your world.

"To increase your body's frequency, you must seek physical manifestations that you can feel. An example of this is the sensation of sand against your feet. This is akin to putting

*your hands and feet in ice-freezing water to help circulate
the blood movement in your body. Take it up a notch and
do a cold plunge."*

-Inder Deol

People who are attracted to similar aesthetics will gravitate
to you. It's also a great way to cultivate your social network
since what you're most excited about will pour out of you.
As an extrovert, this may manifest in the form of talking. As
an introvert, you can energetically attract someone who will
spark conversation and invite you out! Soon enough, you'll
always be in the types of environments you absolutely love!

Like attracts like, so take the time and try to be the version
of you that you see yourself being. Video recording yourself
is super awesome for identifying and eradicating little details
that totally throw off the aesthetic you're going for.

Those two socks and dirty sneakers in your background are
a vibe for someone and a vibe killer for another: you say
tomato, they say tomato (Pronounced "tomaaaato"), but if it
bothers you, get up and remove it. You'll feel much better
with such a small change. Because who you want to be and
who you are is merely an accumulation of deliberate
decisions made consistently.

26. Thrifting

〜

If you've never thrifted, you're missing out on a world that awaits. Second-hand thrift stores are little gems of fashion where you shop formerly owned clothes, paintings, artifacts, and whatever else of people who once bought those things at full price because they saw the value!

Thrifting lets you know what others are drawn to and then fits those pieces into your repertoire. If you're exclusively buying retail, you deal with tremendous markup pricing and a cookie-cutter experience. It's nice to go "off-grid" and pick up items that people will stop you on the street to compliment and inquire about.

Thrift stores in various parts of town will have varying collections, so venture out and be sure to stop in locations in ritzy neighborhoods like Beverly Hills, California, Summerlin, Nevada, and other cool spots in different countries. Thrifting will give you the aesthetic pop you're looking for while being exceptionally reasonably priced.

27. Your Circle

Those who are around you affect how people see you as well. They are a part of your appearance, and it's great to be aware. Just because you become enlightened does not make everyone around you suddenly enthusiastic to dive in with the same commitments.

So, do you still invite your longtime friend to the cocktail party? It's okay not to if you know she will bring down your look, but first, delicately proposition that she too can elevate her style. Certain people fit specific settings, and that's okay. This concept extends far beyond hygiene and beautiful appearance, as impressions consist of multiple factors: social behavior, demeanor, speech, tones of voice, emanating energy, and so much more.

Does your cousin operate under the same social code as you? Consider this when going out with her. When you share mindsets and objectives, it's easier to be aligned when situations require improvising. Still, if you aren't reading similarly or hearing shared information, you likely aren't on the same page.

"Labeling things to a person with a fragile ego won't bring about change because change comes from a place of

power. You won't be able to carry everyone along on your ascent."

--Nana Cheryl D. Elliott

Diversity is important as it helps people grow from being exposed to new ideas, but with some things, you want to be like-minded; when you attract your tribe, you will endure the least friction from judgment. This doesn't mean to keep "yes-women" enablers around who never hold a mirror to your face. It does mean that life requires balance and to remain aware of who you have in your circle.

Certain impressions create particular triggers, and what works in one setting may not be the premier choice for another. Consider going out for live music. Depending on the objective, it would be wise to show off some great dance moves and attract the eye of onlookers, but this is only sometimes the case.

Knowing what's appropriate comes from observing the room and getting a feel for the vibe. Are you surrounded by haters? Will this become a dangerous situation due to that fact? Is this a work party? If your friend starts twerking and getting sweaty, that could work and get you invited to the after-party, but in the wrong context, that could make you look low-class and uninvited to the next soirée.

Context is important. Some friends bring excellent qualities to the table, and you can enjoy places with them that highlight those. Just because you spent so long growing a connection with someone in your intimate home setting does not mean she will fare well in public. In the same way, you are creating impressions to trigger responses in others, you and your friend are also being triggered by the external environment, but not always in the same way.

Your experiences create the framework through which you respond to stimuli, and no two people's experiences exactly mirror each other.

One of you can be shy, and the other boisterous. Just because you have varying personalities does not mean you don't share the same mindset. Being around you can help your friend forget she's shy, and you around her can inspire a bit more reservation. Thus, there is a tremendous potential benefit to your union.

When you get ready to attend an event together, discuss what each is wearing. The outfits should complement each other and be along the same lines in terms of conservative versus classy vs. edgy vs. promiscuous. Since you'll be together for the event, the combined look is just as important as your individual outfits. It'd be ideal to go over these outfits at least a day before the event so changes can be made, as there's nothing worse than rushing to be ready, not feeling good about one's appearance, and battling insecurity the whole time. Whew! Toxic! Inadvertently inviting in the spirit of sadness. No thank you!

28. Preparation

⁓

Preparing your look should be an enjoyable experience. Instead of seeing beautification as a chore, please find a way to make it a part of your hobbies.

If your event is for 7 p.m., consider the beginning of your prepping event to commence at 4 p.m. Play some music, enjoy a libation of your choosing, and get into the zone. Set an alarm that tells you a 30-minute warning, then 15, 5, and 0 (with 5 mins allotted for walking out of the building). Time management is everything; there's no point spending time getting your look together if you miss the whole night.

If you have hired a sitter for your children, plan to have them come before your beauty prep starts, as this is something to be enjoyed as much as the event itself!

The mundanity of life calls for some activities that are not super glamorous, like going to work or grocery shopping. However, if you practice beautifying yourself regularly, you will not only be able to whip up a cute look quickly and with minimal effort, but your baseline level of cute will already be the bomb.

The little actions you take to be the boss chick make a difference. If your laundry is already organized into outfits, what you grab quickly is guaranteed to be fly.

"A classy lady always has her outfits prepped the night before."

—Unknown

Stay ready so you don't have to get prepared at a substantial psychological expense to yourself. The energy of stressing over your appearance can be exhausting, but preparation absolves that. Manifest fashionable people in your life if you aim to be stylish. Not only will they understand when you ask for '5 more minutes!' they'll inspire you to keep up with your fashion standards. Allow yourself to live a soft life by investing in your basic steps with consistency and foresight.

29. Partying and Surviving a Hangover

$\approx$

Drugs are a serious category and topic. It's your body, so it is your choice, and some of those choices can be fatal. Are you aware that trying one drug for the first time could derail your life forever? It's startling to learn, but let the shock empower you to make calculated choices and ask God to bless your plans.

"My parents were pretty open about their drug usage. They told me about what they tried and how that affected them. Those conversations took the allure of drugs away because most stories were pretty bad. I tried weed for a while, but if I could go back in time, I wouldn't have even touched it! It led to me trying other drugs that damaged my skin and led to bad decision-making. I am not a fan of drugs because I have friends who overdosed and died from even trying a drug once! I know even more people who are addicted to painkillers and should go to rehab. It's horrifying, and I want to warn everyone against experimenting."

— Journal Entry, 2023

If you want a thrill, create a new hobby, and don't kill yourself from getting high. Just because you didn't die the first time you tried, it doesn't mean it won't be fatal the next time. Even alcohol is a slippery slope. It's popularized, and especially in college, it seems acceptable to drink on the weekends, but alcohol is seriously a drug. Besides, driving under the influence of any substance can get you arrested and tremendously affect your life. Think about that and say no. If your circle always offers you drugs, stop hanging out with them. It's not too late to change your lifestyle.

The best preparation for partying is the consumption of vitamins and minerals before and after and maintaining hydration levels throughout. Juicing is a terrific way to get nutrients into your body quickly because you skip the heavy digestive processes of solid food. Also, some total meal replacement protein powders tout ingredients that match the required daily vitamin and mineral intake for those of you who absolutely despise supplements in pill form. The point is, if you prepare, your body will feel loved and love you back.

For every shot of liquor you take, accompany it with a shot of water; it's just as effective as juice in cutting the harsh taste of liquor but without the dehydrating sugar content. White processed sugar promotes brain inflammation, so if you can substitute it for something healthier, definitely do so. You should research how to successfully navigate what you're partaking in because it's just that serious.

"Staying up all night dehydrating myself when I had an exam the next day, or doing drugs, stuff like that, was just physically abusive. A lack of proper body management was the issue. Half of my decisions would've been better if I had the proper nutrients to balance my body throughout my party lifestyle. I wish I would've avoided the slippery slope altogether."

— Journal Entry, 2018

When you've slipped into the part of drinking where your room is spinning, and you've already thrown up, here is how to survive the next 24 hours. Hydration is your best friend, and dehydration is the cause of why you're about to feel like absolute crap.

The sugar in your drinks absorbs all of your body's hydration and leaves you to wither; try to avoid sugar and go for water, but the electrolytes in Gatorade will help. If you try to down a bunch of liquids, your body will reject it by sending you hurling. It's best to have tiny sips often or the number 1 choice, ice cubes.

Ice cubes help psychologically and anatomically. The melting ice is a slow drip of a decent volume of water and what your body desperately needs. The crunching and slurping of the ice help center you because it's something you can focus on. Indicators of self-care help you to know everything is going to be alright. Have confidence in yourself and God, knowing you are where you are for a reason, and it's probably to learn a valuable lesson.

You may find yourself sleeping and feel the urge to yack at a certain point in the night. Trust your gut and rush to the toilet because it is coming. Let it all come out, flush, and wipe the toilet if you can because that will give you a sense of a clean slate. The sight of your own vomit will cause you to vomit more. As soon as you can, but slowly, reach for handfuls of water to drink. Not too much at once because, if you vomit, you lose the hard-earned hydration.

Sounds gnarly, right? Why do people even drink? No judgment, but it's hard to accept that this drug is legal for purchase. In British Columbia and several states in the United States of America, there is a legal limit allowing for the possession of many kinds of drugs. Let this be evidence that just because something is legal or accessible and famous does not always mean it's good for you or safe.

Drinking is legal, but getting behind the wheel of a vehicle while under the influence has costly consequences. You may not consider yourself to be inebriated, but a breathalyzer could say otherwise and land you in jail. If you are going to drink, plan to give your car keys to the designated sober person, otherwise remain in place.

Back to this hangover! If you're doing good with your slow and steady hydration methods, it's time to add some bread or greasy food to absorb the alcohol from your system. A tiny nibble is better than no food, so force a bite! Try to give your body a fighting chance at recovery by forcing nutrition. If your leg is cramping up, a banana will cure that by giving you potassium, and for your nausea, lean on ginger ale to calm you. Your hangover can last a whole day, so clear your schedule and be ready to pass out. It sucks to be you in that moment, but it will pass.

"I was very conscious about drugs, and that's why we only used to smoke Marijuana, which I thought was harmless at the time. I heard my friend's mom talk about a neighborhood boy with a bright future who played sports. He smoked some Marijuana that someone had laced with a harsher drug. He was never the same after that. She said he has mental health issues now and roams around the city. She sees him from time to time."

— *Journal Entry, 2007*

30. Nutrition

⁓

Nutrition is so underrated when discussing beauty. 80% of how you look on the exterior can be attributed to what you eat versus 20% to what you do for fitness (and yet, another percentage owed to cosmetic enhancements).

"Man, I busted my formerly non-existent little butt to have a body like this. Waist training was a game changer for having my waistline poppin'! What jump-started a new mentality about my body was having a personal trainer and nutritionist. Sounds expensive, but there are a lot of affordable options. They monitored me during the hard few weeks of transitioning into consistent workouts and eliminating bread and sugar. Then I moved to a beach town where the culture consisted of people working out and showcasing their sexy bodies in beach attire all the time, guys and girls alike. Missing a day's workout was almost taboo. So now I maintain by drinking water, doing abdominal exercises nightly, and watching alcohol intake."

— Journal Entry, 2015

A major driving force for food intake has to do with aesthetics. For many individuals, food's utility purposes are socializing, staying alive, feeling good, and looking great. So many people live for the now and agree to fad diets or whatever their friends are eating, but food choice should be taken seriously as your source for vitamins, minerals, fats, proteins, and amino acids. Do some exploration and look up which health benefits you are afforded from each of your food items. For those with no nutritional value, consider swapping it for something that still hits the spot but will grow your body instead of decaying it.

Cooking can have a sentiment of pressure. Especially if you didn't have someone teach you how to, or you don't find it enjoyable since the food you make doesn't taste that great. If that's you, you're not alone. Some people love cooking; it brings them joy, and they're good at it!

The bottom line, though, is what do you consume, and will it prevent disease, achy joints, and lethargy? How many colors are in your diet? Are you getting enough greens, reds, purples? On an elementary level, those colors can help guide you to diverse food groups to ensure your body is accessing the nutrients needed for proper food elimination.

"We need to talk about poop. Nobody wants to talk about it, but most people have a gastrointestinal situation that is very unpleasant and leads to other problems in the body, unbeknownst to them. The gut is the second brain, but

people eat whatever and expect the system to work itself out. I mean, sure, they're alive, but are they really? The food we're getting these days is filled with pesticides and sometimes even constructed in labs. It's a scary world to live in, and if you're not actively choosing what to eat, it will be chosen for you."

—Lucie P.

Genetically modified food is commonplace, and choosing what to consume is up to you. When in doubt, buy organic. For a food to be labeled organic, it means a certain percentage of its growth cycle was not characterized by extra additives, and it's your best chance at eating food the way it was intended to grow. Wild caught fish aren't exposed to the same antibiotics as farmed fish. Remember, when you consume pesticides and hormones, you're putting that into your body and dealing with the long and short-term consequences.

This can be overwhelming for someone who finds themselves lost in grocery aisles, wondering what to place in their grocery baskets. Here are some tips:

- Shop online for groceries to take your time and not get overwhelmed in the aisles.

- Don't go grocery shopping when you're starving. This will significantly influence your selections, usually in a snacking sort of way.

- When you eat out, notice what you love about your meal, add a mental note for your grocery list so you can pull up an online recipe, and make your own version.

- Follow recipes. If you start remixing things before you're experienced, you might end up with something gross and get discouraged.

- You don't have to make things from scratch to be a great chef; ready-made meals are delicious and save time. Ask your friends and family for simple meal ideas.

- When in doubt, you can rely on meal replacement shakes to get the necessary nutrients. Just read the ingredients and make sure they have the qualities you also look for in your food (i.e., organic, gluten-free, plant-based).

- Identify what nutrients you want, then google food groups that provide those.

- Shop to put together meals instead of miscellaneous items that don't complement.

- Keep a food journal to see what your diet actually consists of and where you can tweak it.

At the end of the day, ask yourself, is what you're doing getting you what you want? The power to change is in your hands, so be the resilient human you are and accomplish what you want!

"One thing about Wealthy people is they really take care of their health. They take their vitamins daily; we're talking iron, B12, calcium, omega's, and a bunch of other stuff. It's not really talked about, but they're doing it. They told me about this anti-aging pill. I started taking it and saw my buddies a few years later. Man! They aged big time, and I stayed the same. That stuff really works, and they don't want to tell many people about it because why increase the competition?"

—Mr. Brooks

Don't wait until you have ailments to start taking care of the one body you have. If you ingest sea moss everyday, you will probably never catch a cold, or if you already have one, you'll knock it out virtually overnight! You're neither an anomaly nor exempt from aging and compromised health, so do the work and keep your vessel authentically in tip-top shape.

Some people have their exterior maintained while living unhealthily and inconsistently. They limit their food intake to stay slim but complain of headaches or indigestion. They have six packs, but their shoulder pops when they raise their arms above their head.

When you know you're taking care of yourself with mobility exercises and proper nutrition, your brain fires with precision, you get results you like, and you're winning.

Consuming sufficient quantities of pressed vegetables and fruit eliminates the need for a fragrance spray to mask odorous pores. Everything on the outside reflects what's happening on the interior, and it shows when you properly maintain your insides.

31. The Big Deal About Organic

~~~

It's imperative to understand what you are putting into your body. If you're so young, you may feel like you have your whole life to adopt a healthier lifestyle later or that you've been consuming a certain way for many years and nothing bad is happening, so what's the urgency?

There's an attack on the food industries worldwide (look it up). Antioxidants help protect your body from heart disease, dementia, type two diabetes, and cancer. A great source of antioxidants is blueberries. One cup of wild blueberries provides over 13,000 antioxidants. But a cup today differs from a cup ten years ago, and that antioxidant count is decreasing. Antibiotics, pesticides, and added growth hormones are commonly injected, fed to, and sprayed over the animals and crops you consume as a part of your diet.

Buying organic is your best chance of eating healthy in this climate because an organic label should indicate less toxicity.

To be considered an organic producer, substantial monetary investments and strict guidelines are required. Fruits and vegetables can't have toxic pesticides, and dairy and meat-producing animals must be raised in conditions that allow for natural behaviors. They are fed 100% organic and not given hormones or antibiotics.

There are some cases of fraudulent organic labels, especially when dealing with foreign imports. There is such a thing as residual toxicity when a farm's soil used to be toxic 40 years ago and still has harmful traces, and then there's the case of contamination from a neighboring non-organic farm. Do you see how complicated clean food can be?

Employees of toxic farms face significant health risks by handling livestock treated with antibiotics, which produce antibiotic-resistant bacteria, then potentially passed to family members. It's hard to come by organic foods in low-income populations where government institutions treat poor people as expendable. The local grocery store in the hood will not have organic anything, and certainly not "100% Organic."

Pay attention to the labels:

- 100% Organic is, as the label implies, all ingredients must be 100% organic.

- Organic means up to 5% of the product may not be organic. Only 95% is required to be organic.

- Made with Organic means at least 70% of ingredients are organically produced.

Please try to always shop organic, although it is more expensive. That avocado may be $2 regularly, and $4 organically, but studies have shown that organic food populations have fewer cancer occurrences.

The gut is often referred to as the second brain. With poor gut health, your hormones are out of whack, your mood unstable, and many symptoms you notice on your skin, mouth, and even your hair are traced back to gut health, all unbeknownst to you!

You can take accountability over what you consume and, at the very least, add the necessary vitamins, minerals, and probiotics to give your brain a fighting chance at keeping you functioning joyously! When you struggle with life's circumstances, control what you eat and drink and increase your supplements for smooth sailing.

32. Weight

~

"We are the only species who do that. In the animal kingdom, males are usually attractive, with vibrant colors and exquisite features. But Human women, we are the prize and put a lot of pressure on ourselves."

-Andi Sage

There isn't a one-size-fits-all criteria for looking good. However, knowing which tribe you wish to connect with is essential to determine what looks good to those constituents.

This doesn't mean you have to fit in, but having a realistic perspective of where you stand is excellent. If your weight feels unhealthy, it probably is. If it doesn't feel unhealthy but looks unshapely and sloppy, it probably is unhealthy. Is this fat shaming? How do you define fat?

Cultures have varying expectations for what looks good or not, some prefer a muscular tone while others call for super skinny, and still, there is 'thick' in all the right places, mainly bootie, and boobs. Pretty privilege is as real as weight discrimination. If you feel shame about being your size, maybe too thin in an environment where all your suitors want Big Bootie Judy, don't fret. First, your eternal Creator in heaven loves you and created you to be you. If you admittedly abuse your body by not feeding it the nutrition it needs, you're not being a good steward of God's perfect creation. You can appreciate being made so prettily by lending your inquisitive nature to learning about helpful wellness resources.

If you have been struggling for years and feeling defeated, there is a way to overcome it! Look at the recording artist Adele's total transformation. If you are feeling shame about some aspects of your look, and you ask a friend if you look okay, it's not fair for them to lie to you when they know, and you know, that some doors will be closed if you don't get your look together! Some people despise conflict and are non-confrontational, but it's rude and inauthentic to constantly comfort someone for their outward appearance when they could use honesty and help!

If weight gain or loss is a sensitive subject, but you still want to get some health in that area, you can contact professional nutritionists and coaches. The central importance is health, but if you want to disguise things in the interim, pay attention to the garments you wear and how they drape your body. Look at people with a similar body type and see how they dress so you can adopt some ideas to accelerate your confidence. You are uniquely created with the freedom to change whatever you want, so don't obsess, just take the initiative.

33. Masturbation & Sex

≈

This next section on sex is just as subjective as the other parts of the book you've read thus far. Decisions regarding sex and sexuality are personal; please only continue reading if you have consent from your guardian.

How do sex and masturbation play into *Hygiene, Beauty and Wellness?* Being stressed about your sexual conduct can affect your mental health, and unsafe decision-making will also endanger your physical health and outward appearance. A basic understanding of your body is empowering; not everyone is taught information at a young age. For example, if you have a yeast infection, the discharge will be a cheese texture, which could mean your sugar intake is too high or indicate a more serious medical condition requiring antibiotics. The consistency of your vaginal discharge varies and serves as indicators that you can compare to online databases.

Many observations are made evident from self-exploration of genitals. Awareness can be achieved through a smell and taste test of bodily fluids. Maybe you need more water, fruits, or veggies, and perhaps you need to lay off on meat consumption. This is not meant to promote masturbation but to draw attention to yourself. Some people reach full maturity and still aren't yet familiar with the shape of their vagina or aware that there are over 20 different looks a vagina can have. Knowledge empowers confidence.

Bodily fluids are produced through orgasm, described as muscular contractions or tension release, followed by accelerated breathing, heartbeat, and fluid excretion. Also known as a climax, this can be achieved via sexual encounters and alternatively vigorous physical exercise, particularly with lower abdominal exercises.

"I was training for a fitness competition in Palm Desert, and when I did the leg raises while hanging from the pull-up bar, I orgasmed in my shorts! It was thrilling and crazy. I felt embarrassed at first, then blessed, haha, and my energy was completely zapped. After training, I took a long nap."

— Journal Entry, 2014

Masturbation is when you create ways to reach orgasm by touching various stimulation points on your body. Sex is when two beings get together and essentially masturbate each other, achieving closeness and orgasm. Some of sex is intuitive, while the rest is technique, and ultimately, your level of comfort with your partner will influence your experience.

"If you aren't fully comfortable being naked in front of someone, you have no business having sex with them."

–Miranda D.

34. How to Approach Sex

B asically and ideally, you'll be two adults in a consensual relationship, preferably married under oath with God, because sex is very special and has a lot of power. Don't let that power defeat you because a lot of people get destroyed by it. Sex as a spiritual union with a relationship commitment from both parties and blessed by God is like building a house on a rock, a sturdy foundation. Alternatively, giving out parts of yourself without a structure of safety places you on a sandy foundation. A beautiful bible reference of Matthew 7:24-27 describes:

"As for everyone who comes to me and hears my words and puts them into practice, I will show you what they are like. They are like a man building a house, digging deep down, and laying the foundation on a rock. When a flood came, the torrent struck that house but could not shake it, because it was well-built. But the one who hears my words and does not put them into practice is like a man who built a house on the ground without a foundation. The moment the torrent struck that house, it collapsed, and its destruction was complete."

The best scenario is when you preserve your sexual expressions and only act on them when you are mature, prepared, and conscious spiritually. Most adults haven't yet achieved that continuously but hope to one day. Marriage isn't the end of the conversation about sexual encounters. Each party must renew their commitment to each other in love, while also committing to the fulfillment of each other.

"I felt so empowered when I bought myself a chastity belt. I knew God was gently warning me about the dangers of having wild lust. Love was beautiful but sometimes led to lust as a runaway train out of control. The chastity belt was symbolic, but I accompanied it with prayer, earnestly surrendering myself to God on this topic momentarily.

It started off hard. Some seasons were easier than others, but eventually, I looked up to the sky and realized that this world is full of love and unlimited opportunities to meet the right person that God has handpicked for me. There's no need to throw myself around in the meantime. Plus, my friend Sara G. recommended I take some time alone, not dating anyone, but doing self-care to the fullest. It was great advice."

— Journal Entry, 2023

35. Out of Control Lust

There is no need to rush into sexual encounters because quality surpasses quantity. You can identify the person who will probably create great sex as comfortable in their skin, not afraid of embarrassment, and a great verbal or physical communicator. This person probably sits in front of a mirror and spreads their legs to see their intimate parts.

Here's a warning about thieves, though. Erections and sexual urges occur all around. When this happens, someone could start an uncomfortable act on another person, knowing they won't say anything and will just get up and leave later.

When you're at a party and you're approached, quickly assess what's their objective, body language, and speech. Most importantly, be aware of your safety options. Your "No's" and "I changed my mind, I want to leave!" Play a significant role, so make sure to use your voice. You also don't want to share your drinks and get drugged unconsciously and taken advantage of. If this has not happened to you, praise the Lord and pay attention. If you are a survivor of a sexual assault, please accept this hug. You're continuously gathering healthy tools to protect yourself moving forward.

This section of the text may seem like fear propaganda. Still, it is only meant to address the severe implications of engaging in lust-filled activities because not everyone respects the boundaries given to them.

"A thief will rob you with the truth. You'll find out later he was a liar."

—*Pastor Kevin*

In sex, you have a powerful voice to discuss what you like and don't like, so don't feel like you have to go along with whatever is occurring. You can, at any point, decide it's no longer enjoyable or conducive to your goals, and that's also okay, even mid-sex.

You can already be in a committed relationship and decide you no longer wish to engage in sex; The choice is always yours. Hopefully, you are with a respectable partner who respects your boundaries. If you are not, it's nice to have legal pepper spray (or other legal self-defense tool) within reach if they respond a little too feral and become a predator. You deserve to feel safe.

If something goes awry, speak up to someone you trust or a voice of authority instead of replaying the events in your head and blaming yourself. There are helplines you can call anonymously and get advice; search online. Sex is a powerful source of energy, and it's beautiful, but it can be misused and lead you towards unsafe scenarios.

Vaginas are portals through which new life forms are brought into the world; let that weight sit with you for a moment. Even if you use a condom, if there is even a little rip, you're risking pregnancy and raising a whole baby, which will completely change your life permanently. It is not easy at all, so preventative measures are crucial.

Masturbation versus sex with someone versus safe sex all offer different experiences. With masturbation, there's no risk of pregnancy or sexually transmitted disease exposure, but you don't get the closeness. If you are touch starved, you can hire a masseuse (not a happy ending) to have some casual touch and release endorphins. Intimacy is awesome for self-confidence, joy, community, and mental clarity, but that's where safe sex takes the cake versus just sex.

Safe sex is when you know your partner has been tested for sexually transmitted diseases, some form of birth control is being used, and you know the person well enough to not risk the pain of being ghosted or used. Ideally, you'd get to know someone through multiple dates leading to commitment and marriage before allowing them into any part of you (mouth, anus, vagina).

Who is their family, what's their history, how do they deal with conflict? Find these things out with a clear head before sexual engagement; otherwise, your truth will be filtered by your new addiction to the person, and you'll create an uphill climb.

"I was well into my adult years when I finally asked my good friend Brittney if I was doing it right. I had sex but felt I was overthinking it. Does this feel good to the other person? Do I look dumb? How does everybody else do it? She told me to move my hips in a figure-eight motion and keep doing that for like an 8 count. She said if I switched the rhythm too fast it was just weird. The mechanics of sex were something I was still figuring out, so honestly the emotional side of it needed to be as stable as possible. I loved my partner and thought that would be enough. But it was so much more complicated than that."

— *Journal Entry, 2011*

36. Energetics Influence Rules of Sexual Conduct

≈

It's essential to re-iterate the phenomenon of energies because they help to explain why safe sex is important. Alpha energy is historically considered masculine, the hunter and giver, whereas beta energy is feminine, receiving and nurturing.

Gender doesn't always determine which is which and can even alternate depending on activities. It's important to know which energy you are operating in at any given moment so you know how to navigate communications during various instances.

The beta is most likely to experience bonding during mating (sex), thus being vulnerable. Without an understanding or contract about the relationship's trajectory and boundaries, it's very easy for beta energies to experience hurt.

Alpha and beta energies do not bond the same way, no matter how 'great the sex was'; this is simply a matter of science. Dr. Pat Allen is a cognitive behavioral therapist who explains precisely how those dynamics work best and which language to use to achieve intended results. If you'd like to delve deeper, you'd want to check out her videos online, read her books, or listen to her radio show recordings. You'll have your mind opened phenomenally, particularly learning the rules of sexual conduct and interpersonal communication based on long-term objectives.

In summary, Dr. Allen describes the loser in communication as evasive, secretive, condescending, and abrupt. If you want to be the cherished one in a dynamic, the other party needs respect in order to be able to cherish you. It would be best if you were either cherished or respected, expecting both means you are a narcissist and have the need to attract a zero who will allow you to walk all over them.

An example of her recommendation is that the masculine energy expresses their viewpoints as, "I think..." while the beta energy should say, "I feel...." Something so simple makes all the difference energetically, and those scripts should be adhered to. If you need clarification on your role, try sticking to one and following the scripts that accompany it.

If your consistency brings about the desired results, great, but if not, switch to the other role. Masculine energies ask the beta how they *feel*, while the beta energy asks the alpha what they *think* and *want*. Dr. Allen suggests that the beta should not ask the alpha how they feel except in an instance wherein they need medical attention or in communicating with male children under four.

Equal communication is competitive, which is excellent for casual friends and making money, but it is a disaster where love is concerned. Doing business during business hours and in separate locations keeps cherished communication intact.

The masculine energy makes an appointment to say hurtful things, cancel plans, or express distaste. They have the courage to say what they want, ask if something is wrong and if it's okay to talk about it, and ask how the beta feels about what was expressed. Particular things like that make all the difference, and it's highly recommended to pursue Dr. Pat Allen's teachings to find out more.

37. Great Sex

≈

People want to feel safe while expressing vulnerability, and what ultimate way to do that than by sharing your desires, breath, and body with someone in a rhythmic spiritual exchange. You'll find yourself skipping along afterward while the pleasure hormones circulate in your body long after the event ends. It's addicting. Love is vital, and being okay with your actions is crucial.

"I can't say that everyone receives a message from God about remaining celibate (No sex before marriage), but I definitely get talked to and often. I've had to work through my guilts and distinguish God's voice from my predisposed trauma. Was it God telling me not to be promiscuous, or was it my fears and unfamiliarity with my own body?

I enjoyed the "Hoe Phase" and the female liberation movements. Both allowed me to numb myself and do whatever I wanted sexually with whomever. But damn, that left me with a disease, a couple of heartbreaks, and a couple of hits to my self-esteem for sure. Some of my experiences were epic, but I wish I could've asked God

about each guy beforehand because some of those I know
he would've said yes to, and a handful were a hell no!"

-V. S.

Nothing is worse than deep agonizing guilt for doing something you were conflicted about, so take your time and breathe. As you tie your soul with someone else, you must be careful who you bond to.

Sex forms a portal for energies to travel through, and some people work out their traumas through that ritual. Imagine someone consciously thinking of something they're mad about, inserting their phallic into you, and releasing it by ejaculation. You can douche the semen, but make sure you also pray over your womb.

The highest forms of love safeguard you against this because if your partner is full of love and the Fruit of the Spirit, imagine the positive impact.

38. Detoxing a Sexual Exchange

To rid yourself of a bad exchange wherein you chemically bonded with a total jerk, the advice is don't see, smell, or hear that person for 6 consecutive months. If you do, the clock starts over again, and you'll be right back at square one, trying to emotionally detox them.

Be deliberate about this action and heal. Talk to yourself aloud with affirmations of, "I forgive myself," "I am not my actions, I am good even if my action wasn't," "I'm perfectly made," "Even my mistakes make me uniquely me," "I am my own best friend!" I won't abandon myself!"

On the physical side of things, to detox a person from your vagina, douche with apple cider vinegar and water. This 'vagina snapback' is a quiet secret amongst sex industry workers who often have to clean themselves on the go. It's called a SnapBack because the combination of those ingredients does wonders to get your flower back to normal while temporarily tightening those vaginal walls! You can also use the recipe for your mouth by gargling and spitting to eliminate bacteria.

When you first consummate with someone, particularly without a condom, their bodily fluids and yours interact to form a new odor. Sometimes pleasant, sometimes not so much, but altogether, unique. Just note the changes occurring in your body and trust your intuition if you feel you need some medicine to help with whatever is going on. Sometimes, you're just not chemically compatible with a person, and even though they are disease-free, your body reacts negatively to your exchanges. You can suggest they use the same sensitive soap as you on their genitals, or even ask them to refrain from using whichever products irritate you. It's your responsibility to communicate what you need.

39. Be Very Selective

One scientist theorizes that each person you have intercourse with leaves a piece of their DNA along the uterine walls, and when you have a child, they embody each of those individuals. That's pretty deep, albeit just a hypothesis. If you go through a hoe phase, the detriment is less about societal pressure of having high body counts. It's more about corrupting your sacred portal.

Most people you'll meet will not be spiritually worthy or sexually skilled enough to enter you, so why discount yourself by enduring? Yes, it's nice to have some sex practice, but there is also something so absolutely divine about the person who is new to sex and amazed by every part of it along the way.

Being turned on or offered nice things is enough justification for some people. In contrast, others want to wait for commitment, the sanctity of marriage, or many other criteria. Be honest with yourself about your objectives, why you seek them, and whether your actions are working or not.

Sex can make babies, and transfer bodily fluids, and it can also communicate what words cannot. When in doubt, remember you can utilize other expressions that give you your intended release yet keep your energy flowing nicely. Like, going to a dance party with your favorite music and going hard! Accomplishing something significant and celebrating with friends; adrenaline-inducing activities like skydiving or doing something for the first time! Or being romantic and holding hands while slow dancing with your partner. Sex is not the only vehicle for pleasure and bonding.

"As I got to know myself, I recognized that once, in the heat of the moment, I tended to go all the way to home base even if I was unprepared with my grooming, which was embarrassing. While on my journey of mastering self-control, I tried deterrents like purposely not shaving my legs or underarms, because I was convinced it would prevent me from going to the next base. That didn't always work, and I would embarrass myself. Instead of frantically digging my heels while descending the mountainside, it was time to start empowering myself. I learned to avoid going to my partner's house after dark or plan activities that avoided intimate settings. Eventually, I just told him I was celibate. It was so much easier to have direct communication.

I became methodical about my regularly made micro-decisions surrounding sex, because peace of mind surpassed any temporary pleasure. It took me a while to arrive at that understanding, and I wish I could've sooner."

— *Journal entry, 2013*

"Every Woman's Battle, Discovering God's Plan for Sexual and Emotional Fulfillment" is a book by Shannon Ethridge. It describes the power of seduction as pale compared to the Holy Spirit, which helps you live abundantly. It talks about the desire to have masculine energy worship you as a form of power and submit to unholy desires that enslave you instead of holiness and purity.

Ethridge writes, "I've known so many women who have journeyed to this depth of desperation, hoping to find something to fill the void in their hearts only to discover that the pit was far deeper, darker, and more lonely than they could have imagined."

She describes romance addiction as a massive interference in life and that the addict can't focus on their activities because of their obsession. This is the power of romance and sex and is not to be taken lightly.

Luckily, God's love is so pure and fulfilling that turning your attention to the spiritual realm will save you from entrapment. You do not accidentally fall into lust; it's a conscious decision made repeatedly. To regain control of your thoughts, you focus on scriptures that empower and educate you:

"Therefore, I urge you, brothers and sisters, because of God's mercy, to offer your bodies as a living sacrifice, holy and pleasing to God—this is your true and proper worship.

Do not conform to the pattern of this world, but be transformed by renewing your mind. Then you will be able to test and approve what

God's will is—his good, pleasing, and perfect will."

—Romans 12:1-2 NIV

Summarizing Ethridge's excellent book would not do it justice, and you are encouraged to explore your own copy. She writes, a Christian woman may have tempting thoughts, feelings, and desires, but she will actively resist and conduct herself according to the image she desires for herself.

Her book discusses how attraction and attention are different from affection, emotional arousal, and attachment, and those are even different from emotional affairs and addictions. They are a ladder and, if unchecked, can spiral out of control. Awareness is an important step, and that is where you are standing. If you seek to further educate yourself, the tools are available.

No one is perfect, but earnest striving toward perfection scores the most points! Healthy bodies are happy bodies. By keeping your health, beauty, and wellness on point, you will learn much about yourself and be in the best position to attract more of what you want.

QUADRANT 4

Coinz

∽

After reading previous chapters, you know how to effectively communicate with people in your network, you've learned to value being inside your body, and you're looking and smelling great! The next slot in your bento box is about making societal progress so you can live abundantly and comfortably financially. You can do a quick search online to determine how to create a resume, apply to school, and other vital skills (check out @wordprecise), but if you want to be truly successful, you'll have to first make sure the machine (you) is well oiled from the inside out. The Coinz section will provide tools to set yourself up for success from multiple angles.

40. Mindset

~~

- When you became an adult you inherited the responsibility of healing your past childhood traumas, but why? You weren't the one who caused the damage.

- Seeking resources to clean up the broken pieces of your heart and mind drastically improves the trajectory of your life. Everyone carries a load, but only you can decide how light yours will be.

- Whether you like it or not, life consists of a series of competitions for resources: For that job position, consider the unique contributions offered by others who compete for the very same seat at the table; although the practice of comparing oneself to others can become compulsive and harmful, to comprehend reality requires a good look around. The person with the lightest load can probably climb the highest without growing fatigued or hitting burnout.

- So, what does lightening the load consist of? Taking accountability for what is in your realm of control and seeking wise counsel to help you delete the rest. You can book therapy, listen to and recite positive affirmations, join survivor groups, and have tough conversations. There are many resources available to heal your heart which is much better than throwing on a bandaid and limping on.

In the context of dating, for every fantasized description you have of a future romantic partner, that person has their own imagination of the type of girl they want to be with. The concept of leveling up to get a man is a great one because what you're actually doing is fixing undesirable traits; you're motivated by the guy or the new lifestyle, but it's actually all about your own journey towards being the greatest version of self that your potential calls for.

If all parents raised children who didn't have to recover from their childhood, there would be no childhood trauma. Reality check- many individuals have obstacles to hurdle over. Some are willing to train and prepare for the jump, while others are comfortably uncomfortable.

It's crucial to realize that a lot of people don't actually care about social justice and equality; elites take care of themselves and provide unfair advantages to their immediate family- it's called nepotism. Sympathetic listeners are a dime a dozen. Are you hoping to be saved by one?

Take confidence in knowing that no one is coming to save you, you must save yourself. Fix your insides so your exterior can shine. It's time to take accountability and elevate.

"Falling happens, but get up, and get up quickly."

–Andi.

Takes lots of reference photos. They communicate a space in time so you can measure your own habits and make adjustments. There may have been a time in your life wherein you operated with the same mindset you have now, yet the results you look back at and critique were lackluster.

Analyze: is the mindset needing replacement or is bolder, more precise execution the answer? Narrowing your focus on your aim does not come naturally to everyone. This ties again to knowing who you are. You'll accept certain happenings based on what you feel deserving of. Sometimes, you'll see an image of yourself, then remember that you had some insecurities with your appearance or even your age, and that held you back from going after exactly what you wanted.

Instead, you settled for something nice but adjacent your desire. Take that same image and look at it a few years later, aw man! You realize you were absolutely perfect back then and must be perfect now with the new tips and tricks you've added to your arsenal. What are you waiting for!! Tell that person NO! And the other opportunity, YES! You can confidently set that boundary because you, honey, have it going on!

41. Optimism

Optimism is the general belief that good things are expected to occur. Optimistic people see that failure is due to some changeable thing and that success is achievable the next time. The pessimist interprets the bad event as something that happened TO them and is out of their control. Subsequently, their negative interpretation influences the expectation towards having no control over their future.

How you respond to annoying or pleasing situations directly reflects your thinking style. The optimist takes accountability, which creates the opportunity for growth and improved outcomes, whereas the pessimist is doomed since she believes in permanent internal causes like low ability or not being worthy. The pessimist will rely on luck instead of taking action.

Beware of women who believe they are victims of other people's actions. Helplessness is contagious! She will never take accountability for her own bad decisions and will always need rescuing. An internal locus of control means your future outcomes are determined by what you can personally do, the changes you can make, and the things you can learn. An optimistic lady will step out of her comfort zone, read new materials, listen to inspiring podcasts, seek like-minded individuals, and practice elevated behavior.

She understands that life is changeable, one micro action at a time, and will make every decision purposefully, knowing they add up to an altered future.

Imagine you're lying in bed, but you're thirsty. Your body odor has been stronger than usual, and your lips are dry. It's subtle, but you know it's better to get ahead of it. The decision you make to get out of your comfortable space and consume a glass of water directly determines your future.

Each moment that you decide to hydrate your body instead of lazily drifting to sleep, you are taking action to change your future. This may seem like a small thing, but this type of thought process happens on a larger scale all the time. Build confidence by being loyal to your own commitments and expectations that you have with yourself. A high-caliber woman believes in her own ability to alter situations. Take control of your destiny by owning your decision-making process and watch your beautiful life unfold.

How you operate in response to life's circumstances is predicated by your mindset: With an elite mindset, dialogue and understanding are achieved instead of arguing and strife. There's no need to prove your points to others, as every interaction should instead be an opportunity for learning. For example, becoming offended about political topics only reveals small-mindedness. Understand that the world shakes and moves to the rhythm of the money trail; at the root of most social issues is a financial standpoint. So why let someone's personal view ruin your day?

Racism is offensive, but you don't have to let it waste your time. The racist has an impoverished mindset and uses race to boost her self-esteem. She does not understand that network is net worth; thus, another culture is something to learn from and sell to.

There are bad apples who marry into elite society while carrying their poverty mindset, but they do not represent the majority. Some men will knowingly marry a woman with a poverty mindset because they rationalize that access to her father's network will be worth it. She is tolerated and avoided but not revered. Self-control and elegance of speech will always outrank her in the long run.

Another characteristic of the elite-minded woman is the observation of the most frequent thoughts she carries with her. She'll honestly assess them for their impacts:

Positive

Negative

Serving

Hindering

Elevating

Descending

She'll apply the same valuations to her speech, actions, and emotions. What does her speech sound like? What does she want it to sound like?

Elegant

Optimistic

Melodic

Witty

At first, this discipline will feel restricting, but it's simply a boot camp with great rewards. Eventually, you will see results, and your default reactions to life's circumstances will become characterized by stoicism, grace, and class.

Trade in shock, disappointment, and sadness for amusement, adoration and intrigue.

By noting micro details in herself, she will easily identify them in others, making her a master of perception. She will be able to discover and fine-tune all aspects of her being so nothing about her is unrefined, thus achieving her level-up aspirations.

When observing other women for the purpose of emulating them, it's best to comprehend their true context. If you are copying someone who dresses like a party girl, shares revealing images, and leads with sex, make sure you two end up in the same place. She may enjoy a better outcome, but why?

You may think you two are equals, but if she comes from a rich trust fund home and you don't, she may be able to get away with a lot more than you. Don't let the example of the few lead you into error. Do your research before making someone your role model. When you move deliberately, you will be one step closer to becoming the you, you aspire to be.

42. Deliberate Action

Expecting the *Coinz* aspect of your life to prosper by relying only on your charm will get you exceptionally far. You may think it is because of your uniqueness, but mostly, it is owed to your investment of time and strategic improvement to fine-tune your skills.

'Charm' is defined by Dictionary.com as "a power of pleasing or attracting, as through personality or beauty;"

Ideally, your charm and ability to charm should be progressive and fine-tuned. This is not a natural occurrence and instead requires self-analysis, measuring success vs. failure rates, studying other charming individuals to emulate their strategies, and a willingness to abandon flawed methodologies to make room for the adoption of new ones.

"I think of life as a wonderful play I've written. And so my purpose is to have the utmost fun playing my part."

— *Journal Entry, 2008*

Whatever you do, let it be deliberately immaculate, but without overthinking. While you're training yourself to do things a particular way, yes, a lot of thought goes into it, repetition too. Olympic champions spend countless hours perfecting their crafts, but with that type of work ethic, their baseline is raised, and even on a bad day, their performance is superior to the average athlete.

Think and plan, then let your brain relax; When the feeling to take action occurs, take immediate action right in the moment! This is the secret to getting things accomplished. Trust yourself and walk confidently with the skills you've acquired and an expectation of favorable results!

"Dance like no one is watching; email like it may one day be read aloud in a deposition."

--Unknown

Sometimes, it takes sheer willpower to do a relatively simple task. The delays are seemingly insurmountable. You read about varying learning and performance disabilities, like ADD (Attention Deficit Disorder), and wonder if that's what's holding you back. If you're too tired to work on your project but then spend an hour cleaning and organizing, your procrastination indicates self-sabotage.

Sometimes, not trying at all seems much better than trying your hardest and failing, so you stay in that space of not trying and identify yourself as a procrastinator. Really, you're just afraid and slowly turning into your biggest hater and sabotager. Force yourself to do something, and consistently do it during an allotted time every single day. By 30 days, your brain will have formed new pathways reinforcing the action, and you will be light-years away from your avoidant behavior.

If you have been avoiding something for a long time, the next time you get an impulse to do it, stop everything and go do it! Ride the wave of your emotions and impulsivity. Then have a huge celebration for whatever action you took. This can be jumping up and down and hollering, or looking in the mirror and congratulating yourself exaggeratedly. The wins will propel you towards the next impulse!

It's important to act right away because your behaviors and habits have a comfort zone. When you step out of that comfort zone, your survival mechanism will bring you back into comfort. This works when you're dropping below achievement and also when rising above. The brain doesn't know the difference, it just knows its uncomfortable. It's your job to force action, and what better way to do that than to ride your own wave of energy, right in the moment. As a reminder, remember to celebrate those tiny wins every single time! There is no glory in comfort, only through forceful action will you ever see sustainable change.

43. Work Ethic

If you rely solely on motivation to accomplish a goal, you may never acquire it. Deliberately forcing yourself to do something is how it gets done.

If you struggle with attending events on time, you can make excuses or set multiple alarms to help you count down to departure. If you're not good at studying, you can hire a study coach or watch free tips in online videos. Becoming successful means experiencing discomfort repeatedly until you reach your destination.

"Who cares what your actual goal is, but it better be big and scary. You break it down into pea sizes until it looks like your objective is being approached. If you're lazy, commit yourself to doing a piece daily. Get up and have that drive to take one step, which turns into a ladder that develops into a staircase. Structure makes that possible."

—Miranda Dean

If you think you can circumvent the grind, you're wrong. When that grind has an ill effect on you, it's the equivalent of a check engine light coming on. Observe your self-care and make adjustments so you remain balanced. Pushing yourself to exhaustion may be necessary sometimes, but if you repeatedly operate with that design, you will experience burnout.

At the same time, expect fatigue. Most fantastic results require sacrifice. You're going to suffer in one way or another, either from wasting your life away dreaming about the life you want, but not actually living it. Or, by putting in the work, a lovely pain resulting in an elevation of your craft, career, education, mentality, or social and financial status.

Understand that what you are committing to has a time limit, and fully investing in yourself will birth tenacity and a courage you can carry with you as a badge of honor.

Learning new vocabulary, identifying architectural styles, and adopting foreign cultural nuances are all forms of success. Success really depends what you feel the need to accomplish to feel fulfilled. Whether it's bodybuilding, embarking on parenthood, earning a degree, or working in the career of your liking, you will be required to focus and remain consistent throughout your success pursuits.

If ever you falter and don't complete what you set out to do, it will mean precisely that. You did not finish. While excuses are in abundance, results are what actually matter. Time waits for no one; if you sit around, it will pass you by. What are you waiting for?

Your *Coinz* is your hustle, a measure of your progress and track record of achieving milestones. It's too easy to create the illusion of progress, and people are starting to catch on to that. What you see on social media is curated for the audience, but a real grind is measured by consistent action and results. You can say you want to be an author, but if you don't continuously write pages until reaching 'the end,' you won't become one.

Write down your start date, and add a new date for each time you work on your goal. You'll notice your trends of effort. Sometimes, you may have a flurry of activity followed by weeks of nothing. This is all good information to see so you can identify your strengths and weaknesses.

If you have lived a life of lazy efforts, it's time for a rebirth. Your past does not have to be your future, but it will be grim if you don't initiate the change now. If you are already consistent and work ethic is your strength, congratulate yourself, because staying at it is more than half the battle, and you're doing great.

"It's not about quick, forced change, but it is a process of constant development and re-evaluation. Life is like a tanker. You can't turn on a dime. There's so much accumulated throughout your life that you either take with you or must drop if you set out to change something. That's why it's not a simple process to decide to do a 180-degree turn and just be done with it. Especially if you want the change to be substantial."

-Roger Enz

44. Your circle

Don't confuse dating someone successful with you being successful yourself. It's essential to connect with other individuals who inspire micro changes; If you're wise enough to leverage your relationships to upgrade yourself, your success can be measured in many ways. As short bursts of time pass, you can potentially evolve tremendously.

There are so many beautiful attributes to be added simply by constantly absorbing and mingling with the people you aspire to be more like. Such things as monetary wealth, class, language abilities, personality traits, articulation, outward appearance, spiritual grounding, aptitude, resilience, and many others can fit this space. One person can bring what another person doesn't, yet it works out because it's what all parties need.

It's enjoyable to join forces with someone with a grander lifestyle than your own. As long as you don't try to keep up by straining yourself financially, and so long as you're not ego-driven jealously, your mind can be expanded exponentially. Be ready to observe and willing to ask questions, and you'll see that just by being associates or friends with those individuals, your life begins to elevate! It also goes in the other direction when your network offers much less. Who you choose to be around will influence you, so if you have friends who don't have excellent work ethics, be sure to balance that out with people who regularly grind towards their goals. You don't have to abandon people with low performance, but you may notice a natural shedding as you grow.

Discover and become confident about what you bring to the table so you don't experience imposter syndrome (feeling like you don't deserve all bestowed upon you).

An abundance mindset will get you far and attract others who operate in abundance. Hunger is an admirable trait because it shows you're willing to go after more. Desperation, however, is a red flag and low vibration.

Desperate people are ready to take the scraps off your table when you aren't looking and also lower the market values with their "accept anything, please!" behaviors. You can be humble and still anticipate the best of the best. Contrarily, keeping your eyes lowered to the ground to not ruffle any feathers prevents you from seeing what's at the top.

45. Mentorship

≈

"Some of your best life lessons or hacks will come from books. Now imagine what you may gain from being best friends with the people who happen to become their authors."

— *Journal Entry, 2021*

A mentor is someone who has lived the experience you're interested in and teaches you the fast-track version so you have fewer pitfalls and are on route to achieve even more than them.

Attracting a mentor is like discovering the cheat code to life, to which you won't be disappointed. Mentors like pupils who are willing to grow, show measurable progress, and have a hunger for what they desire, who, quite naturally, feed the ego of the mentor. In exchange for bestowing their great wisdom upon you, they get to hear themselves speak and relive some of their most invigorating experiences. They love you for the mirror you place in front of them, and you benefit from this in magnanimous ways! Sometimes, they will introduce you to other like-minded individuals who can assist you on your path, and sometimes, they might only be available by phone to decipher what problem you're faced with and offer great counsel on how to navigate it.

"When the student is ready, the teacher will appear."

—Ina Ferrera , Life coach

Ask the Creator to bring you a mentor, and they will often appear in the most random settings yet be with you for a lifetime. You never assume they will be in your life forever, as some are only for a season. Never take their communication with you for granted; remember to be present for every precious interaction.

Sometimes, you'll have 'aha' moments throughout the entire visit. Other times, you may only want to write down one thing and even still have instances where the conversation wasn't particularly enlightening. You are still benefitting from the energetic exchange of being in the presence of someone who wants good for you, which is truly priceless! Asking someone to be your mentor is a bit of a coin toss, but why not ask!

Alternatively, you can gather roundabout and soak up the nuggets of truth while your relationship with them evolves organically and increasingly. You never forget someone who teaches you something; it's one of the most underrated gifts to secure a mentor!

"Sara G. changed my life. We met in an undergraduate course. She was so pretty and did not dress down. Even if she wore a hat, it was one with sparkles and glam. A lot of my style came from her, but what I loved the most was her wit! She was never caught off guard with any comments because her sharp mind already had a sophisticated rebuttal loaded. In one phone call with her, I'd learn like 12 life lessons that she just saved me time and energy.

I never asked her to be my mentor, but she 100% was! When we went our separate ways, I noticed my decision-making became questionable, especially about men. Should've stuck beside her, but ugh, that's life!"

—Journal Entry, 2012

"Auntie Jackie and Aunt Felicie were great women to call because they were cool enough to understand my dilemmas, and had intriguing examples from their own lives to back up the advice. I feel blessed to have family who I know I can trust to have my best interest at heart."

— Journal Entry, 2022

46. Networking Pitfall Advisories

～

You may only sometimes be the mentee of your group. Sometimes, you'll be the one who has more to offer to someone who befriends you, hoping your level will elevate theirs. Contributing to the human community is excellent, and when the right people are matched, it provides self-actualizing benefits for all parties. Beware of the pitfalls mostly tied to connections not based on a shared definition of love.

Love is truly the answer as it measures conduct. You will know what and what not to do intuitively if your heart leads thoughts and actions, but are your instincts sharp?

"Siri, what's the definition between Instinct and Intuition?"

—- "Instinct is a biologically natural behavior. For example, when you put your hand on a stove and immediately pull away because it's hot, that's an instinct. Intuition is a feeling inside you. "

— Journal Entry, 2019

Instinct is an innate, fixed pattern of behavior in response to certain stimuli, which can be derived from a poor example.

If you've learned from someone through direct or indirect observation, your choices may be hardwired in a self-harming way.

It's important to have sharp instincts by training yourself to notice and respond to red flags and positive glimmers. Some people will ride your coattail straight to the top, which is not always a terrible thing, but you shouldn't be weighed down and exhausted from the laborious task of fork lifting them either.

Action-oriented speech is nurturing, like adding vitamins to a shake. You can hang out with someone who talks the talk, and because you know they make constant forward (and measurable) progress, you are fed by their banter. Empty ambition, however results in jealousy, and jealousy is very dangerous.

The easiest way to filter for potential jealousy is to align yourself with others achieving more than you. Con artists and scammers can fake a perception. Learn to identify potential haters. If you have someone who likes your aesthetic and often copies you but rarely or never comments on it by praising you, that's a hater. If you have someone who tells you they want to be just like you, also be careful because they may want to take your spot.

Gravitate people with abundance mindsets who will never see the table as only having one seat available. People who regularly celebrate each other, if only in small gestures of speech, are awesome. At the same time, if you are seriously pursuing something and the competition is high, don't share that opportunity with a friend who might also audition. This is a matter of preserving your own self-interest while also having love for members of your circle.

If you constantly need to self-protect around people in your network, you may want to find a new tribe. Leading with love is the ultimate freeing experience, and if you can't do that, understand the reality of that sacrifice. You may determine that the person you are around has something of value for you to gain, and it's worth enduring the relationship. It would be wise to remain clear on your objective so you don't accidentally make yourself vulnerable to having your boundaries dishonored.

Please ensure the trade-off is worth it because you are damaging a part of your soul by being around them, with effects that are sometimes instantly apparent but may not surface until much later.

"I was a model. When we pulled up to the club, my friends lingered until I worked my magic to get us all in for free. I had my own little walk, and this demeanor was expressed by body language that said, 'I expect, I receive, I own, give me.' I met a guy and committed to a relationship with him. After a few years, I came around my former friend group, and they expressed concern. "You used to be so confident.

Are you insecure now? What's going on with you?" They were right. I was constantly doubting myself, averting my eyes from contact with strangers, and really heady. How did I get here?

His constant "realist" opinions about me and my aspirations covered the mouth and eyes of my dreamer self. I started believing in his limiting perception of my abilities as if they were my thoughts. Whew! Now that I'm free, I can breathe again. God's scriptures tell me who I really am. I have a royal identity, created in God's image and capable of flourishing in absolutely everything I desire. 5 years later, I'm finally back to being ME!"

— Journal Entry, 2022

Some interactions come with a price that isn't worth paying, regardless of what you could potentially gain. It all comes back to boundaries. Go forth with armor, and the moment you discover it is penetrable by negativity, remove yourself from that situation and pick up to burn that ugly seed before it takes root! You'll eventually become so great at identifying toxicity that you will get a whiff of it and sprint the other way. If you're not at that point, let these words incentivize you to get there faster.

You deserve better, will receive better, and will be okay once you separate from that negative source. It isn't always easy, but liberation is worth more than the finest jewels.

47. Separating From A Provider

"Don't let your left hand know everything the right is doing."

–Wendell

When separating from a source of financial support, be strategic and give yourself a soft landing. Soft landings are so important for the preservation of your mental health. Research your options for housing, supplemental income, and food. See if you can store away small cash reserves and spend with your projected departure in mind. You may have to sacrifice some of your lifestyle, but it's only temporary, with an important goal: FREEDOM.

When you react emotionally, you are near-sighted and most likely to cause yourself great distress. (In cases of violence, this advice does not apply, as sometimes things are a matter of life and death!).

Shelters are often depicted as shady places where you can be robbed or sexually assaulted, but many of them are actually not! Some have dormitory-like settings, are very clean, and have lots of resources introduced to you by dedicated staff who do this for a living. You don't have to rough it alone, as you are not the only one in your position!

And maybe your circumstances are not so extreme, but you're taking the leap to leave a toxic job. The security you nestled in for so long hindered you, and you are ready to bounce! While you still have that job, schedule interviews at other places and don't mention it to your co-workers, who may accidentally gossip about your plans. When in doubt, be in touch with your intuitive self and strategically propel yourself to new heights, but when you tells yourself to leap, you better!

The problem with sticking around for too long is the amount of shedding you'll require later on. You'll have to shed off that layer of heavy junk you've allowed to pack into your mental and physical space for so long. When you remain long after an experience's expiry date, you're not being faithful to yourself. Meanwhile, you're increasing internal distrust, which could lead to semblances of low self-esteem. Do a cost-benefit analysis, and be honest.

If you're planning a soft landing and it's not quite ready, find a way to reframe your mentality in the current situation. If your days are dragging on, you are dying on the inside, so spruce things up. Rely on other spaces in your bento box to propel your energy, change your lip-gloss color, adopt a new food item into your diet, or spend time visualizing your new future.

What kind of music does this new you listen to? What does she wear? You can adopt some of those features into your now by adding an extra bounce to your walk or walking up to a stranger and striking up a conversation. There is no need to be miserable when a shift in mentality and a slight adjustment to your routine can liven up your world! Tomorrow is not promised; if you live through a challenging time expecting to one day be happy, that's really taking a gamble. If you cannot shake the emotions surrounding your situation, please reflect on the Relationship with Self chapter of this book and perhaps couple it with a cognitive behavioral therapy session. You don't have to stay stuck. With nurturing and empowering support from resources, you can choose another option. Look at you, go!

You've got this, and here are some scriptures to give you reassurance along the way:

"As I walk through the Valley of the Shadow of Death, I will fear no evil. For you are with me."

— Psalm 23:4 NIV

"Blessed are the poor in spirit: for theirs is the kingdom of heaven."

—Matthew 5:3 NIV

"Rescue me, Lord, from evildoers; protect me from the violent, who devise evil plans in their hearts and stir up war

daily. They make their tongues as sharp as a serpent's; the poison of vipers is on their lips. Keep me safe, Lord, from the hands of the wicked; protect me from the violent, who devise ways to trip my feet. The arrogant have hidden a snare for me; They have spread out their net's cords and set traps for me along my path. I say to the Lord, You are my God." Hear, Lord, my cry for mercy. Sovereign Lord, my strong deliverer, you shield my head on the day of battle. Do not grant the wicked their desires, Lord. Do not let their plans succeed. Those who surround me proudly rear their ugly heads; may the mischief of their lips engulf them. May burning coals fall on them; may they be thrown into the fire, into miry pits, never to rise. May slanderers not be established in the land; may disaster hunt down the violent. I know that the Lord secures justice for the poor and upholds the cause of the needy. Surely the righteous will praise your name, and the upright will live in your presence."

–Psalm 140 NIV

48. School

Education takes many forms, and you should take advantage of any that speak to your style. Some people read books, listen to podcasts, watch performance arts or television, and some take online courses while others are on campus. Your brain is capable of growing, depending on your active input. Take an interest in something and let its exploration take you down a tunnel of intrigue. It can be anything, but spend time learning about it and then practice explaining it aloud. You don't necessarily need someone to listen, but hear yourself! You'll see where you need to seek more clarity when you listen to yourself fumbling over details aloud;

Active brains are sexy. If you are not interested in becoming smarter for the sake of knowledge itself, do it because it will open doors for you. In interpersonal relationships, what a bonus you'll be if your pretty other spaces in the bento box also have some intellect to match.

Start by looking up current events in the news and picking something somewhat interesting to you. Practice naming the main points aloud, and when you're ready, bring it up at the dinner table to your friend. Keep it short and straightforward, but offer a snippet, and you'll be surprised how that may influence the conversation and, at the very least, the other person's perception of you.

Knowing what's happening in the world around you will also affect how you interact with people, offering you a level of empathy and self-awareness that will, at the very least, help prevent you from making social plunders.

When actually in a school setting, think of the long play when you consider dating a classmate. Will you start ditching classes to avoid them if it doesn't work? Cuties may cross your path, but what is helpful for success is creating a network of classmates who can help you with complex assignments, help lighten the load by agreeing to work in teams, and even give you hookups on who can write your paper for you if you're in a time crunch (like services @wordprecise provides). Even in online class settings, you can still reach out to the email list provided by your instructor and, as an icebreaker, ask who is interested in sharing notes. You'll be surprised how hopeful others are for the same connection.

School settings have a vibration. When like-minded individuals work towards a goal, even being in that environment will positively affect you. You're not alone if you're intimidated by writing or mathematical processes, studying, and note-taking. You can be taught how to master all those things if you open your mouth to ask for help. Material things can be taken from you, but what you learn cannot. Exercise that brain of yours. It's something you won't ever regret!

49. Instructors

- The best defense against being brainwashed by a professor, author, or mentor is critical thinking. There are courses on critical thinking offered, but if you're going to teach it to yourself, hear this: Every thought you hear has an exact opposite belief, and you should compare and consider both. It's great to be open-minded, but even better to examine what you hear or see, investigate the information from other sources, and then draw conclusions. You score points for actively evaluating input rather than blindly following.

Teachers and mentors have strengths and imperfections, so never undervalue your opinions and perspectives. When the person you are learning from covers topics related to marriage and abundance and is operating in lack, you may not want to hold their advice so closely to your heart. Yes, failure does teach a lot, but you also want to hear from people who have excelled in their areas of expertise rather than just acquiring a degree (unless the topic is how to navigate school).

Studies that present information for you to read and adopt are written by people. If an academic describes the privilege afforded to pretty people (pretty privilege) as toxic, yet she is not pretty, you may want to guard your mind. Someone with an abundance mindset will teach one set of understandings, and a scarcity mindset will, by default, teach something else. This applies to subjective studies, whereas math and chemistry are straightforward and consistent.

It's great to form a relationship with your professors the same way you would a classmate. Attend their office hours, ask questions, and be courteous, which could result in earning a mentor who will teach you things even once the course is over. They may even introduce you to people in their network who can help you in your emerging career and write you a letter of recommendation.

Building rapport with your professor is beneficial in multiple ways, including favoritism during grading, so you can know how much to trust what your educator is teaching you. You are the gatekeeper of your own mind, so use wisdom and protect what comes in.

50. Workplace Dynamics

- Workplace culture has its own nuances. Be clear about your objectives, lead with love, and guard your heart with critical thinking and intuition. In some cases, when you enter a new job, there could be passive aggression so subtle that you think you're going crazy with how often you experience gaslighting. Gaslighting is when someone antagonizes you but pretends like you are making it up in your head. Being the agreeable, nice one does not always serve you, as the sharks at your job will use that against you by pushing up against your boundaries until you fold into tears and frustration or quit altogether.

- Backhanded comments and criticizing you in front of your boss are all micro-aggressions, along with scapegoating and letting you be the fall person when projects don't go well. Sometimes, you can set a boundary by telling them you don't appreciate the behavior and want them to stop, but most times, those people are intentional about their undermining and won't let up. Your strategy should be to stay calm, have quick, witty responses practiced, and be ready to throw back at them.

A bully won't target a potential bully, so strike back, but never get caught by your boss. Never yell, but be assertive and firm in your voice; you can raise it slightly louder than the other person. Micro-aggressions at work do not improve on their own. It would be best to stand up for yourself; going to the boss is not always the answer. If you become a nuisance to your employer, you will be viewed as the problem, so address those bullies head-on.

You can look up videos on how to deal with workplace bullying to further this point. Just don't remain the victim because you don't have to! Remember, you don't have to associate with people making you feel miserable; if you decide to, don't let small things slide and grow into more significant problems. There is no need to fight unprovoked, but don't be too agreeable. You will have happier relationships when you put your self-interest first.

With everything in life, interpretation is up to the eye of the beholder, but your influence on the narrative sends some message. In any situation, when you're the new girl, you will automatically attract haters and friends. It's just how life works.

On your first day of school, work, or as a new church member, be mindful of how you carry yourself and what you choose as attire because whatever you can't maintain will be noted by onlookers. Judgment is real, and although it'd be great to live in your own oblivious bubble, it's better to be aware and grounded in reality, even if you wish to pretend you're not. Aloofness is an excellent strategy because it allows people to reveal their moves with less precision since they think being stealthy isn't necessary with such an unaware victim. In this way, though, you attract sharks.

If you're a supervisor, people look to you for leadership, so own that role and be a leader in many ways. How you walk to the break room, how well you hold eye contact while speaking, and the type of beverage you sip during meetings all paint a picture of who you are; that image is what people carry home with them each workday.

Know how to work the room and assume everyone is gossiping about you (even positively) behind your back. Be sensational and explicit about your own objectives. Is it to move up in the company? Do you have intentions of making this job your career? Will you need that professor to write a recommendation letter for you? Are you hoping to evolve your role to a hybrid position so you can travel the world while still making paper? Focusing on your aim will bring you closer to your desired results.

Power dynamics are important to acknowledge and utilize. When someone is in a position of power, you want to maintain a role of esteem towards them. If you reveal that you covet their spot or have a means of usurping it, they will treat you like a force that needs to be squelched. Instead, feed their ego by being a good little pupil, meanwhile collecting gems of knowledge that increase your value.

The best way to feed them is to bring something to the table, whether an inquisitive ear or something unique about you that tickles their fancy. People in positions of power often understand the power of manifestation and likely willed you into their atmosphere of existence. They appreciate you being there, see your value, and love you.

"Think of the people in your circle who are interested in speaking to you and love you. You may assume that they're around simply because they are your family members or you happened to cross paths, and it just works as a default.

Well, no. The reality is those people are around you because you're amazingly awesome. They can't get enough of you! You're not a casual coincidence. You're that spark! Own the fact that you're special. Not everyone is, but you? You definitely are."

–Richard Greenwood

51. Trusting Your Team

≈

*"Doing things on your own strength means you don't trust
God, and consequently, you have a void of peace."*

—Karla Pascacio

Trust is a choice. Choose how much trust to give
someone, dive into that, and enjoy the experience. If
you're constantly on edge, waiting for something terrible to
happen so you can be prepared, then you have an ungraceful
existence.

Create a space to operate in peace by trusting yourself to take
appropriate self-protecting action should something go awry.
Mitigate losses by using discernment when deciding how
much trust to allocate to someone, but once you offer a
degree of trust, do it fully! Enjoy the freedom within that
space, and experience every detail to the fullest because the
next moment isn't promised, and you deserve full moments.
If you expect trust to be earned, you're on the pessimistic
lower half of the glass, hoping someone pours into it to reach
the fill line.

A team member can be related to your job, community
service event, church choir, school project, or any other co-
facilitation. When your success relies on the efforts of

another person, that makes you a team member. The sooner you view it that way, the more intentional you can become about nurturing the relationship.

Being of the mentality that 'work is work' and relationship building is inconsequential will make your life much harder. You are not a boat in the middle of the sea but a fleet. Rely on the skills and life experiences of others to add to your own capabilities.

An extension of this concept is to be the iceberg above the surface of the cold blue water. There's a whole other half to the magnanimous iceberg, which is wholly submerged yet still solid ice and heavily impactful. You can be a part of a team yet still be the shining star by maneuvering yourself into those positions.

Volunteer to be the one who emails the document to the professor. Your name will stand out; be the first or last speaker in the PowerPoint presentation so your impression can be made on the collaboration. Take credit where credit is due by finding ways to elevate yourself amongst a crowd while still maintaining that their contribution and worth are essential.

In some cases, attracting the most attention in the room is a valuable tool and can be accomplished with simple adornments. Shoes with a little bell that jingles as you glide by, a butterfly hair clip to complement an otherwise plain outfit, and a hair flip on the way to the washroom. Little gestures like these denote influence and power, but sometimes, flying under the radar is better.

For people who are diamonds, a little bit of dirt will not distract from their shine, so even if you want to lay low, there's a certain level of you that you have to own. Suppose you and your buddies enter a public space and engage in prohibited behavior. In that case, you will be the one who catches the eye of the loss prevention guy watching their security camera footage. Everyone was not created with equal features, so don't think what goes for someone else will be the same for you.

Be strategic with how you decide to reveal some of your unique qualities. Scope the situation and ease in so you can take others by surprise, not vice versa. Do you speak the language that they're using? There's no need to flaunt that just yet. Let them think you don't know what's up, so when the timing feels right, you blow them out of the water.

When conflict arises, that's okay. The competition itself isn't destructive; it's responding negatively to the conflict that is the problem. Many people are conflict-avoidant and see non-confrontation as being a great trait. Consider that conflict means there are varying viewpoints, head-butting each other gently with the potential for achieving a new understanding.

All parties stand to grow and learn; by pursuing a resolution, you become vested in the process, thus achieving increased commitment.

52. Financial Literacy: Expenses and Budgets

Your financial goal can be quite different from your friends, and it's essential to know this so your spending habits won't mirror theirs when you all go out for the night or on vacation somewhere. Peer pressure is real regarding wanting to appear a certain way and doing whatever is necessary to keep up with that appearance.

Comedian Kevin Hart once described how he was a millionaire hanging out with guys richer than him, and he was spending what they were spending so he wouldn't look broke. He lost so much money that way and quickly learned to stay on his own path.

Do you want to have enough *Coinz* to party for the weekend, then make that money back so you can do it again? Do you want some of that money put to the side so you can start to save? It's important to understand expenses and budgets.

To determine your expenses, observe how much that weekend cost you and break it down into an itemized list: Gasoline $_, Outfit $_, Party Entry Fee $_. Now, you know what is required to fulfill the entertainment part of your budget. Your budget is how much freedom vs limitation you must spend to meet your expenses. What about the rest of your expenses? Rent $_, Carwash $_, Dinner with friends $__ , Groceries $_, Gym Membership $_.

The list can go on and on, and what's great is that writing out those figures will reveal to you how much you allocate and allow you the opportunity to make some changes. This may seem simple, but you'd be surprised how many people don't know how much money they have coming in and are quite unclear about where it goes

You may want to increase your Party Outfit fund. You can now deduct from the other expenses to remain within budget. A budget is meant to help you keep track of your spending so you aren't surprised or stressed as the days and weeks pass. They encourage you to set a spending limit and try your best to adhere to it.

Budgets also tell you if your job or gig brings in enough revenue. In this day of the Internet, you can look up side hustles to supplement your income, so don't shy away from understanding your money just because the dollar amount may not impress you. With good accountability going on, you're being a good steward of your cash.

Every dollar counts if your financial plan is less about living for the day and more about creating savings to purchase something in the future.

Knowing exactly how much money you have and how much you'll need in cash or in your accounts to make sure your bills get paid is such a boss move. The empowerment you feel knowing you have specific purposes for those dollars spent will allow you to make better decisions regarding your consumerism. This places you even more in the driver's seat. You will be more in control in deciding what events to attend or the quantities of things you want to buy. Add your bill type, amount owed, and payment method to your calendar and set an alarm or reminder.

If you have a bank account, getting slammed with overdrafts or insufficient funds fees is no fun! You lose money in large quantities, and for what reason? Lack of foresight, no, ma'am, it's time to change how you operate your cash.

(If you have any overdraft fees charged from the bank, call and request that several of them be reversed. Explain that you can only pay off the balance if given some reversals. They are obligated to do this for you.

Reviewing your bank account transactions from the last month is good to see how much you spend on what. See if you can create categories of things, so if a couple of transactions are from different food establishments, they can all be grouped into one category and do the same with other similar transactions that can be easily grouped.

If you identify where you can cut some spending, make those adjustments; if you are okay with your spending but need a little more money to cover the expenses, that is a great insight. If things are just right, then feel great! Knowing what's going on with your finances feels good and should be practiced daily, weekly, or monthly.

The benefit of investing your money in life insurance policies, stocks, and real estate is that you can make your money work for you instead of just holding on to it and having it sit in a bank or shoe box. There is some risk because the bank could technically go belly up and leave you empty-handed, but without risk, there is no reward.

"The general rule of investing is to have your investments in more than one place."

–Aleleh

When you put your money in accounts that accrue interest, your wealth is growing, and you can find ways to avoid paying taxes on your beautiful bounty. Or imagine you still have long-term plans of going on your dream vacation. Look how much it will cost you, and then see where you can discipline your monthly spending to save.

You may tell yourself you will cancel your gym membership for a year and work out at the beach instead. You don't have to commit to a life of deprivation, but it is wise to set short and long-term goals and place some spending on hold to reallocate funds to something that will be a remarkable moment in time for your life's story.

Are you an impulse spender? It's a real thing. Sometimes, you may even be a shopaholic and not know it. If you feel the drive to go shopping anytime you are dealing with feelings of melancholy or loneliness, that indicates a problem. Look up ways to deal with that; otherwise, you will find it challenging to meet your financial milestones, thus perpetuating the cycle of sadness and more spending.

Be around people who are great with money, and these are often the ones who drive modest cars and wear non-labeled sweaters. Still, some flashy people only spend small percentages of their income yet live lavishly because their incomes are so high. Money can be a taboo topic for people, but don't be afraid to ask someone successful for tips on their relationship with money.

"What I thought I knew about finances was completely wrong. I met Edward YaYa, a real estate investor, tax lawyer, and boxing promoter, among other titles. He introduced me to the book, 'The Millionaire Next Door,' which explains where you are on the wealth continuum, what your spending habits say about you, and where you and your future generations are headed if you emphasize consumption. I never felt so poor, haha, but that was a great starting point for understanding money. He shopped at Walmart because he owned Walmart stocks. I went from desiring designer brands to learning that 90% of

millionaires spent a maximum of $17,900 U.S. on a motor vehicle. I was mind-blown. And forever grateful. My first stock purchase was because of his influence."

—*Journal Entry, 2018*

Tell yourself that money is attracted to you, is always coming your way, and loves you. Never say that you're broke, "financially on the light side at this moment" is an excellent way of saying you're out of funds, but 'broke' is a mentality you want to steer clear of in action, thinking, and speech. Positive money affirmations work since everything, including financial abundance, comes with mindset first. Then, what follows are methodical steps towards your financial goals.

53. Time Management

~~~

"I've been writing this book for months, and with two sections remaining, the deadline keeps pushing further and further away. My business partner pushes me forward on the road to success and attainment.

My writing comes from real-life inspiration, quotes taken from real people who are casually introspective. Geniuses in all humility. This was my circle. I realized that I was losing inspiration because I stopped spending time experiencing new things. After all, I was busy writing.

I needed those physical sensations of awesomeness found in my surroundings. I needed to feel that often, but even without it, I needed to push forward rhythmically, consistently, and relentlessly. What's one day in 365? Stagnation if you're waiting, failing if that's your excuse. Triumph if you get up, get out, and get something."

— Journal Entry, 2022

Everything in life has a rhythm. Breathing, blinking, walking, eating, and many other automatic yet recurrent behaviors.

Judgment to the side, observe that you are highly consistent about whatever it is you do. When you are ready, to be honest about your addictions and patterned rhythms and behaviors, you'll be empowered; even if that honesty reveals that some terrible things should be alleviated, self-awareness is a mighty tool for forward movement. Accepting your reality will help you exercise walking in harmony, even when the details may suck.

Some things can throw off your rhythm, requiring a jumpstart to reignite your motion. Such events are debilitating changes in physical health, injury, emotional turmoil, and primarily the HALT, as mentioned earlier (Hunger, anger, loneliness, and tiredness). If you allow those things to destroy your rhythm, it doesn't mean the rest of your life stops flowing. You become stagnant, your laundry and dishes pile up, you have valid excuses, and you become a failure. But you don't have to stay there for any determined amount of time.

Push forward even when you're not inspired or feeling well. Doing one thing towards your goal daily is still considered progress; doing nothing for any day is the opposite.

"Success is as much about timing as anything else."

–TD Jakes

There are seasons for relentless tenacity and seasons for soft living. Once you know which time you're in, you'll have a clear trajectory for prioritizing your actions. A lack of sleep can be carcinogenic, so you'll want to be aware of how much rest you need to keep yourself healthy, but if you're in the season of grind mode, push yourself to go hard, knowing it's not forever.

Inspiration is for amateurs. Professionals show up every day and see what happens. Showing up creates the potential for opportunity. Show up daily as your whole self, aware of your environments, noticing entrances and exits, what the person at the front desk was wearing, not the color of a person's eyes but the lightness compared to the darkness.

Become in tune with the world you interact with and exist in so you can own that you are a mini architect placed on earth to construct a favorable reality for yourself and your constituents.

You and your talented brain have a purpose here, so bring your top-notch game, operate on all cylinders, and give it all you've got! The same dedication applies to restful periods.

"'Ahh, tomorrow is Shlomi's day. He doesn't give a f about nothing.' I have to have days where I do whatever I want, where nobody asks for anything. I love it."

— *Shlomi*

When you are in your period of rest, do so entirely! If you can't turn your brain off, place yourself in an activity that requires being fully present, like a strenuous hike, competitive sport, hot yoga, karaoke, and perhaps even a prescription from your healthcare provider to help alter your state of mind temporarily.

Whatever timing you're in should be honored because it is through time management that you will accomplish what you set out to do. The same applies to goal setting. Earlier, you learned the difference between a goal and a dream were actionable, measurable steps. Don't just project them somewhere into the future. Give yourself time projections for your efforts and completion dates for end goals.

When you miss the deadline, don't just casually glide past it, and don't be bogged down with anxiety. Instead, create a new deadline! A woman who never cares about time cannot achieve the *Coinz* she sets out to gain. Accomplish things by managing time, then give yourself bouts of escape to paradise where the sun's rising and setting connote pleasure and spiritual freedom, away from the hustle and bustle.

54. Commanding Life

"Just because you're alive doesn't mean life will go right for you; you have to actively command it and have that attitude and expectation that things will be on point. Even if there is a setback, I know it's just for now. You gotta see things spiritually, then you will have foreknowledge of what will happen. Otherwise, you're always surprised. During the worst month of my life, I asked why is God doing this? He encourages us to read the bible to find out. So, when I read the book of Joshua, it was entirely about being courageous. "Be of good courage" means getting out there and accomplishing, not sitting around passively."

–Lydia Hardee

Even the act of manifestation requires concerted effort. It would help if you cast down thoughts that steal confidence in your dreams and organize your environment so that everything reminds you of where you are intentionally heading. Things start to click into place harmoniously once the wheels are turning, but willpower is required in the beginning, self-control all throughout, and faith weaved into every crevice.

If you are still determining what you want to do career-wise, start with volunteering or working for pennies in fields that interest you. You may wonder how to achieve great wealth with a minimum wage or nonpaying job, but it's all about curating your experiences so your dreams begin to chase you, not the other way around.

Through doing things you're passionate about, who you are created to be will become more apparent, and opportunities will emerge. In the meantime, be fully equipped as a favorable candidate when they come your way.

These days, the internet offers a plethora of information and free courses. Teach yourself the basics of a foreign language, take a handwriting class, learn Microsoft Office programs, or something else. Anything you can add to your experience will prepare you for your upcoming objectives.

Find what you love by exploring who you are, and watch how quickly money comes flying at your face! You'll watch your problem evolve from needing more funds to rejecting income sources that need to be aligned with your purpose and identity.

"Manifest what you want to manifest by choosing the seeds that will germinate. Then, you don't have to wonder about the outcomes you're encountering. I'm extremely selective about which seeds to plant into my soil."

–Dr. Dewaina R. Hardee

55. Vanity

- Whenever you chase money, it can't find you. Long ago, a person stayed at their one job for their entire career, like the elders born in the 1940s. People explore, juggle, and trade in their employment experiences because the 2020s call for liberality and exploration. Flashing constantly on social media platforms are the glitz and glamour of ordinary people who struck it big seemingly overnight. Oh, how alluring, yet deceptive.

"'Vanity leads to downfall.' My father is an eloquently spoken and brilliant man. Well-versed in biblical knowledge and beyond. He's said many profound things, and this simple statement carried the same weight. He was right. I began to observe myself making decisions based on how my hair looked, what I was wearing, and what effect I wanted to place on others. I became aware that vanity led much of my decision-making; I consciously changed that after that."

— Journal Entry, 2023

Vanity as a driving mechanism for your pursuits might look like working hard enough to level up and then stopping once you get the desired attention. Flexing on people, showing them the incredible new level-ups you got, opens you up for losing some of your momentum because your energy was expelled flexing so hard; it also makes you susceptible to haterism, a powerful energy force that people can inadvertently or consciously project towards you.

When you are en route to flourishing, why create unnecessary opportunities for people to dim your shine? A way to avoid that is to develop a fellowship community with those who share your values and generally love you.

Examine your own heart for its motive before you present information. With the right audience, you will garner support for your projects and progress, which can propel you to new heights. If your network shares what you're doing with others, potential new business may come your way.

As with everything, always be conscious of yourself, which will give you an advantage in a world full of self-consumed mentalities.

Conclusion

- What a delicious assortment of spaces you have in your Bento box. Like humans as complex beings, these inner workings all come together with fluidity.

- It's incredible to think of all the processes that must occur in the body to even take a bite of food. The births and deaths of cells, constriction of blood vessels, and traveling of neurons along myelin sheaths. So much of it is automatic that you rarely take a moment to appreciate, let alone educate yourself on minuscule yet urgent details.

- Ideally, you'll want your bento box sections to work together similarly. No matter what they are, optimal efficiency requires more focus and concerted effort.

Faith, believing in unseen things, will get you far. Love will keep you clean with the right type of dirty. Awareness of self, Christ, and your obligation to humankind to lead with love in all your endeavors will give you a life worth excelling in.

"You get to know yourself in the struggle. You get to know God better, realizing he is your ever-present help. You become aware of the excessive things and people in your life and appreciate your blessings. Struggle gauges your

*level of commitment and qualifies you for paradise
experiences."*

—Daniel Hardee

How many people forfeit their blessing because they refuse to fight? The caterpillar goes through the process of metamorphosis, in which it changes from a robust little worm into a beautiful soaring butterfly. Some of your mindsets birth a desire in you to cut the struggle short. You don't want the cocoon to be properly weaved around you, always trying to look too far ahead. Allow your eyes to be covered to meditate within instead of robbing the caterpillar of its destiny. The baby chick pecks out of the egg, gaining the strength to survive and thrive in its new environment.

Take the time to invest in the four quadrants of your life, and you will experience fulfillment and joy while also, by default, teaching it to others. Emphasis on the joy part! Things will start to click into place in beautiful, miraculous ways.

If you dedicate your life to Christ, seek communities (including online) that will help nurture you along your path. God has already equipped you with all you need, and you'll gain more sweet gifts along the way. This is because he loves you specifically and handpicked your talents for today.

Hygiene, Beauty and Wellness, Coinz, Relationships with Others, and Spirituality are massive enough categories to spend your whole life organizing and fulfilling. Seeing that they all deserve your nurturing and maintenance is a starting point for arranging how to approach that dutiful job of pursuing excellence in all domains.

Balance is important; too much time in one area will mean insufficient time in another. You decide which needs more investment at any given moment since seasons do change in that regard.

You'll notice that your dedication to your spiritual being will be your helping guide through the ebbs and flows of the other categories of your bento box. Wisdom is a gift; without it, a fool will always squander all of her earnings, so what would be the point of organizing your hierarchy of importance if God is not at the top? He gives you the wisdom to shower your other quadrants with blessed favor.

You matter, and if you've reached the inevitable end of this book, then you must believe that truth, too. Continue to invest in yourself because when you shine, you, too, become a mentor to others just by living and loving your truth.

THE END.